BOLIVIA
in Focus

A Guide to the People, Politics, and Culture

Robert J. Werner

Interlink Books

An imprint of Interlink Publishing Group, Inc.
Northampton, Massachusetts

First published in 2009 by

INTERLINK BOOKS
An imprint of Interlink Publishing Group, Inc.
46 Crosby Street, Northampton, Massachusetts 01060
www.interlinkbooks.com

Library of Congress Cataloging-in-Publication Data
Werner, Robert J.
Bolivia in focus : a guide to the people, politics, and culture / by Robert J. Werner.—
1st American ed.   p. cm.
ISBN 978-1-56656-299-7 (pbk.)
1. Bolivia—Civilization. 2. Politics and culture—Bolivia. I. Title.
F3310.W47 2009
984—dc22   2008050156

Printed and bound in Korea

BOLIVIA
in Focus

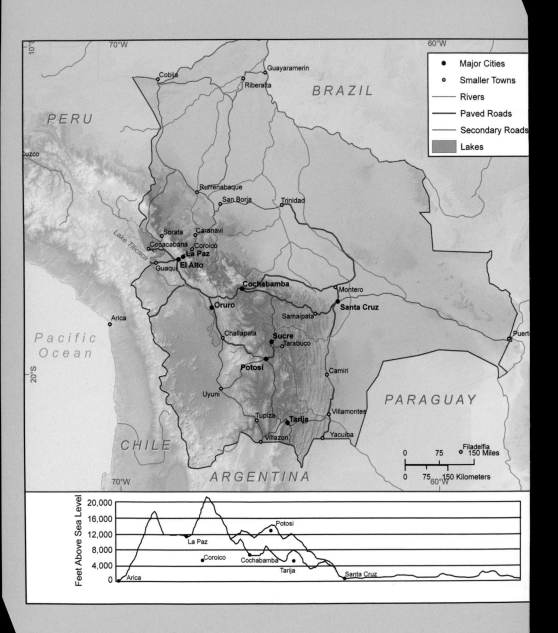

Contents

Introduction

A LAND OF CONTRASTS

Bolivia was an unlikely country from the beginning, with no natural borders or cohesive identity. All of the country's borders were difficult to establish—Bolivia fought wars with every neighbor and lost land to all of them. The consequences of this weak sense of national unity lie heavily on the country.

Geographic and social fissures divide Bolivia. One is the highland west compared to the lowland east. Not only does the physical geography and resource base differ between the two regions, but historical ethnicities are quite distinct and there is a gulf between attitudes. Many highlanders favor socialism, especially the large indigenous population who want state control over natural resources. Easterners have a more mixed ethnicity and tend to be laissez-faire. They see themselves as economically dynamic and resent the taxation and control from the faraway *altiplano*, the Bolivian part of the high-elevation north-south basins extending from Peru to Chile.

A second fundamental divide is an ethnic one. Bolivia's demography is unique from all its neighbors, with the highest proportion of indigenous population in all of Latin America. These native people have historically been marginalized, with their lands taken, their labor commandeered, and their participation in government denied. Some subsist in remote villages, far

Multicolored Bolivia, the town of Alota. Image © Morton Elm

from roads and the modern economy. The quality of schools and health care is minimal. The overall result is that the country faces serious development problems. Ethnic differences are reflected in a deep urban/rural gap and conflicting political and economic philosophies. Income is much higher in urban areas, and while the country as a whole has low levels of education and health care, rural areas have vastly less. The social fabric of the indigenous is often quite different from that of Bolivians of European descent and mestizos, as it is based on traditional values of land ownership and labor allocation that are frequently inconsistent with European structures of government, private property, and a competitive economy. Economic class disparities are the fuel that ignites Bolivia today. A traveler to Bolivia, via a book or in person, must understand the country's turmoil, which often leads to strikes, marches, and street protests.

A third split is one in ideology—a conflict between socialism and market economics. A traditional, mostly white, urban upper class generally favors capitalism and foreign investment, while labor unions, miners, and the indigenous typically prefer socialism. They fear that Bolivian natural gas will be the last resource they have, and that if foreign companies exploit it the way they did silver and tin, Bolivia will be left with nothing.

All of these tensions are exacerbated by Bolivia's politics. If political instability is measured by coups and attempted coups, Bolivia holds the world record, averaging one every 10 months over 125 years of independence. The country's stormy political history is an important reason why it has the lowest levels of economic development in South America.

Despite the country's deep problems, there are many winds of change. The laws of Popular Participation in the 1990s have brought the indigenous into politics at all levels of government. They have helped empower women, requiring a third of the slate of nominations for elections to be women. Albeit with rocky politics and street protests, the country has been democratic since 1982. Bolivia elected Latin America's first indigenous president in Evo Morales in 2005, who has been empowered by the indigenous, unions, and a sense of nationalistic protectionism, fueled by windfall government revenues from a booming natural gas industry.

No matter what one's political and economic philosophy is—to favor open markets and foreign investment or nationalistic socialism—Bolivia is a country to watch. If this, the poorest country in South America, can channel gas revenues into development, and if they can find the balance of power between an old oligarchy and a large indigenous population, then they stand to find some degree of social justice that has been missing since the arrival of colonialism five hundred years ago.

For the naturalist in each of us, Bolivia offers soaring Andes, adventure treks, and ecotourism. For our curiosity of history, the country provides a complex web sure to amaze even those who have read widely. Bolivia's captivating archeology serves up endlessly amazing sights, from the majestic ruins of Titicaca and Samaipata to the little bits of ancient pottery strewn all over the Andes. For culture seekers, the carnivals, music, textiles, archeology, and artisan products have vivid regional color, depth, and variety. But perhaps the main reason to love Bolivia is Bolivians themselves. Willing to share their rich and complex society, the visitor will find a cordial and warm people open to answering questions and welcoming your curiosity.

Fernando León, in Calacala

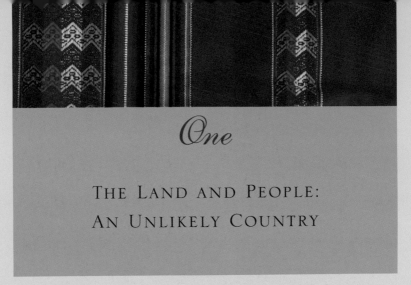

One

THE LAND AND PEOPLE:
AN UNLIKELY COUNTRY

*N*ature's imprint on Bolivia created marked differences in lands and people that challenge the country's sense of national unity. The geographic divide between western highlands and eastern lowlands separates distinct landforms, climates, vegetation, and natural resources. Cultures, ethnicities, and attitudes vary by highlands and lowlands too.

Western Highlands and Eastern Lowlands
The western highlands, with an average elevation of 12,000 feet (3,650 m), comprises just over a third of the country. They include significant deposits of sliver, zinc, tin, and a host of minerals used in industrial processes. Their climate is dry and cool and supports crops of *quinoa*, a native grain rich in nutrients, as well as wheat, barley, beans, and potatoes. The highlands provide good grazing land for llamas, whose meat and hides are essential products of native cultures.

This physical geography is important because the highlands are the traditional core of Bolivia. This was true for native civilizations, which developed a well organized system of agriculture that included extensive trade with coastal Pacific areas. It was true during colonial times, for it was in the highlands that the Spaniards found their precious silver and gold. (Bolivia never had large deposits of gold, but had enormous quantities of silver.) The highlands supported a higher population of more organized societies.

They produced more and had better infrastructure. They became the seat of political power.

The eastern lowlands lie at only a few thousand feet of elevation (a few hundred meters). Their resource base is quite different, having few minerals but large deposits of oil and gas, resources completely lacking in the highlands. The climate in the northeast is part of the humid Amazon rainforest whose wetlands are often only accessible by rivers. The southeast is called the Chaco, a sparsely populated, arid land with a unique ecology. In between are crops of soy, corn, and beef, production quite unlike the highlands.

People and attitudes are different too—highlanders are called *Kollas* and lowlanders, *Cambas*. Separate cultures evolved in these vastly different lands. Kollas are largely descendants of the Inca and Aymara. The Inca did not conquer the humid, flat east, so when the Spanish took over, their territorial edges were similar. But because these far away regions were frontiers, both the Inca and the Spanish had limited influence. The east was colonized from the east, up the Paraguay River from Buenos Aires, with an important Jesuit influence. Geography and history worked together to give the east different native groups and a separate political evolution.

Kollas have a political orientation that derives from their geography. Mining in the highlands strongly fashioned the development of the country's economy. Mining led to labor unions that became, and remain, powerful players in the country's politics. Unfortunately, silver brought almost no benefit to Bolivians, tin only a little, and the nitrates of the Atacama were lost to Chile. Many highland Bolivians believe that the oil and gas deposits in the east are the country's last chance to build wealth from their resources, so they support state ownership and development to ensure that benefits accrue to Bolivians instead of foreigners.

Cambas too have a political philosophy that reflects their geography. They want to export their resources to the world without control from highland politicians, so taxes and profits from oil and gas are a major political issue between east and west. Easterners feel considerable frustration by the fact that the traditional seat of political power lies in La Paz and Sucre but the money to be made lies in the east. *Cambas* see themselves as economically dynamic but ignored and undervalued.

Topography itself conspires against national unity. East-west travel in Bolivia is difficult. The Andes descend steeply to the east, resulting in plunging gorges through which few roads exist. The country has only 2,000 miles (3,200 km) of roads, of which a mere six percent are paved. A comparable area in the sparsely populated western United States has 12 times more paved roads. The few roads that do span the landscape are often far from villages that have access to the world only by paths through rugged mountains or steamy, dense rainforests. Roads in the wet east can become endless ribbons of mud with heavy rains, bringing all traffic to a halt for days. Agricultural products in remote areas sometimes rot before they can be brought to market. The challenge of reaching markets leaves people subsisting on the land, hardly participating in the monetary economy at all. It is difficult for the government to provide health care and education to these remote hamlets, further contributing to deep rural poverty.

Given the fundamental differences between east and west and the powerful influence that complex topography and varied climates have on the country, it's worth a closer look at the physical geography.

Climates, Soils, and Vegetation

Highlands and lowlands result in very different climates. Highland climates are primarily influenced by elevation. The *altiplano* is cool throughout the year because of the high elevation and is dry most of the year because the cold ocean current and resulting winds coming from Antarctica are usually not strong enough to push humidity up into the mountains. The exception is from December to February when they do, and the northern highlands experience a wet season. Occasionally, wet Amazon air makes it over the Andes to produce destructive floods and landslides that

Fields of the altiplano, with the majestic Andes range in the background
Image © Frederic Roux

kill hundreds of people. Massive erosion from catastrophic rains can be seen in La Paz and scattered as far as the Atacama Desert in Chile.

The principal influence on the lowland climate in the northeast is winds from the Brazilian Amazon. These winds are humid all year, but bring even more moisture from December to February,

when an already wet climate becomes drenched. The Chaco in the southeast, a unique assemblage of climate, soils, and vegetation, is not influenced by the Amazon, so is usually arid. It is typically hot, except when southerly winds blow up from Antarctica during July and August, when temperatures can drop near freezing.

All of Bolivia is near enough to the equator that there is little seasonal variation in temperature within any one region and sunshine is very strong throughout the country. Bolivia has only two seasons—wet and dry.

Soils and vegetation vary by elevation. Highland soils are generally thin but become productive when irrigated. Cold temperatures dictate crops of small grains, beans, and a vast variety of potatoes (the International Potato Center in Lima holds 100 wild species and 3,800 cultivated ones). Hot temperatures of the lowlands lend themselves to soy and corn. Natural vegetation is also quite different according to elevation. Sparse highland vegetation consists of low grasses and bushes. Lowland vegetation in the northeast is that of a rainforest, while the Chaco is covered in spiny desert vegetation.

Geology

Geology is essential to understanding Bolivia. The South American continent lies on a tectonic plate of the same name that slowly moves west. It collides with the Nazca plate that moves east under the eastern Pacific Ocean. The result is a subduction zone where the Nazca plate slips underneath the South American plate, which crumples, creating the Andes. Earthquakes and volcanoes are consequences of this plate friction. Mineral deposits are too. The compression and heat that result from plate convergence cause minerals to re-form in concentrated bands of folded rock. The combination of pressure, heat, and deep hydrology concentrates mineral ores into rich veins that have altered the course of human history in Bolivia.

Silver and tin were the most influential minerals. The discovery of silver at Potosí in 1545 drew the Spanish conquistadors into what is now Bolivia. Potosí produced half the silver of the New World from 1570–1650. It opened up trade between Europe and China because silver was the preferred currency of the Chinese. As silver deposits became exhausted, Bolivia was fortunate to make an immediate transition to tin in the early 20th century as international demand for tin cans boomed.

But Bolivia has many more minerals, including lithium deposited in the enormous dry salt lake beds of the southwest that are called *salares*. Each *salar* was created as the highlands rose and cut off the flow of rivers to the ocean. Rivers then flowed into basins that formed huge lakes and evaporated, leaving salt-encrusted depressions, some of which contain lithium salts used in batteries. Bolivia exports antimony (used to flame-proof paint and ceramics), bismuth (the main ingredient in Pepto-Bismol), quartz (for electronics), and borax (a water softener, cleaner, and used to make glass), as well as copper, gold, lead, tungsten, and zinc. Bolivia is physically landlocked, so the country's mineral exports are often more expensive and less competitive. Despite that fact, minerals are central to the country's economy, accounting for 40% of exports. (Bolivia is not economically landlocked after a free-trade zone was created in 1992 at the Peruvian port of Ilo.)

In the lowlands, natural gas and oil deposits were created by the deposition of vegetation in shallow depressions that were covered by eons of sediment whose weight and heat metamorphosed the carbon into gas and oil.

The same geology that created Bolivia's mineral resources caused the disparate and complex landforms that led to centuries of headaches trying to figure out the country's boundaries.

Formation of a Country

Bolivia is named after Simón Bolívar, the Colombian liberator whose armies swept south to defeat the Spaniards. Bolívar wanted a united South America but didn't get it. During Spanish times, the two seats of power on the continent were Lima and Buenos Aires. Bolívar's generals thought that Lima and Buenos Aires would fight over border lands, and convinced him to create a buffer zone. While Bolívar didn't want there to be a Bolivia at all, the country was not only created but named after him.

Establishing the borders of the new country became a long string of problems. Many of the lands had not been explored or demarcated. Argentine maps showed one border, Brazilian maps a different one. Peruvian and Chilean maps differed, and Bolivian maps gave yet another account. Bolivia would struggle to claim its borders from independence in 1825 until 1904, when a peace treaty was finally made with Chile. Each quadrant of borders posed a unique set of problems.

The Bolivian–Chilean border

Northeast

The tinder for border problems in the northeast was encroachment by Brazilian Portuguese in the 1880s, lit by a rubber boom that made it suddenly matter where the border was. Brazilians were more enterprising than Bolivians in exploring the Amazon basin. Most expeditions from Bolivia failed. Roads were non-existent and rivers were torrents down thousands of feet of rocky elevation. While Brazil's rivers flow to the central Amazon, providing a unifying transportation network, Bolivia's rivers flow outward, creating centrifugal force. Bolivia's two major rivers that flow to the northeast, the Madeira and Mamoré, descend through eighteen major rapids in a very complex topography. The British *Charge d'Affairs* in 1853 called the northeast the "Siberia of Bolivia."

Bolivia previously had found no reason to take an interest in the northeast. Rubber tires were introduced to the world in 1895, causing an explosion of activity in the western Amazon basin, presenting insurmountable problems for Bolivia to exploit this new wealth. There were no roads from the Bolivian highlands and the area was largely settled by Brazilians. No borders were marked. By the time Bolivians tried to erect markers, Brazilians were already settled upstream. Brazilians attacked and took a Bolivian province for their own when Bolivia tried to tax the rubber. There was no Bolivian government in the area, so the Bolivian rubber baron Nicholas Suárez had to raise an army of his own.

The American Colonel George Church attempted to build a railroad that would connect the rubber-producing regions to the east. It was a disaster. Labor was in short supply. Church's company had to convince the Bolivian government to stop sending prisoners to add to an already-inefficient labor force. The company could not deliver proper equipment to the workers, who were plagued by malaria, tuberculosis, beri-beri, blackwater, and yellow fever. Valerie Fifer, who wrote an authoritative book on Bolivia's borders, describes the workers' camp a few years after the start of the project:

There is now nothing to show but a slight scratch in the ground—representing the first cutting—a house, a few rough sheds, some cleared land, two wrecks in San Antonio harbour and several great heaps of the cases of tinned meats and broken bottles.

Church's locomotive was later found in the jungle with a large tree growing out of the smokestack.

Ironically, Church's railroad was completed just in time for the world price of rubber to plummet. Brazilian rubber seeds had been planted in Ceylon and Malaya. The price of raw rubber went from three dollars a pound to seventy cents just as the railroad became operative. So Bolivia lost a province in the northeast and it would still take years of treaty-making with Peru and Brazil to establish Bolivia's northeastern borders in the Amazon jungle that Fifer describes as a "boundary-makers' nightmare."

Southeast

The southeastern border with what is now Paraguay was long ignored because the climate was severe and the few Chiriguano and Toba natives who lived there were hostile towards the passing Europeans, as were the jaguars and tigers. There were virtually no resources in the Chaco. Cattle could graze after clearing the thorny forest, but they were far from markets. Quebracho trees produced the chemicals used for tanning hides, but this was not a source of wealth. Both Paraguay and Bolivia struggled to find any outsiders willing to settle in the Chaco so that each country could lay a stronger claim to the land. They tried settling Belgians, Japanese, Americans, and Russian and German Mennonites who came via Canada and Mexico.

Spanish maps showed various borders with Paraguay. As with all of Bolivia's borders, there was little cause for anyone to figure out where the borders were when it was all Spanish empire. As the empire broke apart, the lack of resources and people in the area did not provide reasons to draw borders. The southeast was so much of a backwater that it was functionally independent of the Spanish empire. The Inca were not successful in subduing lowland tribes because people there were nomadic hunter-gatherers, without the settled agriculture that the Inca needed for their systems of social control. After taking over the Incan empire, the Spanish found the limits of their control to be similar to the Inca's.

The Chaco remained largely unexplored until well into the 20th century, and physical geography provides good reasons why. Besides the absence of resources, sudden rainfall over the flat land of the Chaco results in rivers that often flow into vast, complex swamps. Seasonal temperatures go well above 100° F (38° C), drying the swamps to reveal extremely few water sources.

Hopeful to find access to the Atlantic that they could call their own, in 1844 Bolivia mounted an expedition to explore the Pilcomayo River that drains the most southeastern part of Bolivia. English carpenters were hired and the expedition was led by another Englishman named Masterton. Three boats were built in Chile, disassembled, reassembled on the Pilcomayo, and launched. They managed to cover only thirty miles in thirty-seven days, when they ran aground in sixteen inches of water. Valerie Fifer describes the conditions the party faced:

> Depths of as little as four inches lay ahead, but even while reconnaissance work was being undertaken, sudden floods surged down the river and all three vessels were completely wrecked. Carrying their wounded, for the crews had been continually harassed by Toba Indian attack, the survivors limped back on foot.

The Pilcomayo would largely be forgotten until the Chaco War finally brought the whole southeast into a national crisis.

But Bolivia's big push for access to the Atlantic was to the river Paraguay, whose northern reaches were part of Brazil and whose eastern bank was held by Paraguay. Bolivia always had legal access to the river Paraguay, even before the Chaco war of 1932–35. Bolivia had lost its coast to Chile in the War of the Pacific in 1879–1884 and became keen to push over Paraguay as a scapegoat for problems at home, to declare a victory that would raise national pride. Even after Bolivia lost the Chaco war, it still had legal access to the river. Bolivians built Puerto Suárez in the 1880s, named after the rubber baron Nicholas Suárez, though it was on a backwater of the river that suffered seasonal dryness. One of the jobs of soldiers stationed at Puerto Suárez was to go shovel out the millions of rotting fish left behind when the waters receded.

Having fought the Chaco war to get access to a river they always had access to anyway, Bolivia tried building a railroad across the part of the Chaco that remained in their hands. The railroad still operates today, but at no time did it ever carry profitable trade, although there are hopes for it now. After losing 50,000 soldiers, the war brought an economy on its knees to flat on its face, and now humiliated too. Bolivian access to the Atlantic turned out to be nothing worthwhile after all.

Bolivia's other big problem in the southeast was Argentina, primarily for reasons of 19th century Argentine threats to Bolivian sovereignty and 20th century Bolivian economic migration to Argentina. Bolivia's relations with Argentina were always rocky. Argentine armies entered Bolivia on four occasions. The first was in 1810 when the city of Cochabamba rose against forces loyal to Spain and in support of Buenos Aires, which had recently liberated itself from both Spain and Britain. The Argentine army was at first welcomed throughout the Bolivian *altiplano*. However, it soon became clear that the Argentines had no intention of creating a separate, free Bolivia. Bolivians in the cities revolted against them within a year, but it was the loyalist Spanish forces from Peru who threw out the Argentines.

After pushing the Argentine army out of Bolivia, the royalists continued on into northern Argentina, where they were defeated by an Argentine army under the command of Manuel Belgrano, who then brought his army back into Bolivia, getting as far as Potosí before being driven out again by the royalists. A third Argentine army entered Bolivia in 1815, again to fight against forces loyal to the Spanish crown, and again they were soundly

City of Potosí

defeated. The Argentines saw fit this time to empty the royal mint at Potosí on their way out. Soon after, a fourth Argentine incursion into Bolivia under José de San Martín finally helped liberate Bolivia from Spain, but only after Bolivians broke their alliance with San Martin and sided with generals under Simón Bolívar instead, leaving the Argentine army no choice but to go home.

Relations with Argentina worsened in the 1930s when Argentina sided with Paraguay in the Chaco war. Argentine efforts to mediate the war were conducted by the self-serving Argentine diplomat Saavedra Lamas, who sought credit for ending the war, but who wrecked several promising negotiations that could have ended it years earlier. In the 1980s, the cocaine-dictator Garcia Meza invited brass from the Argentine military to Bolivia to help construct a military regime and teach thugs how to conduct "disappearances." Argentine advisors were thrown out in 1983.

Bad relations with Argentines persist now because hundreds of thousands of Bolivians live in Argentina as economic migrants causing some hostility, including periodic violence against their Bolivian neighborhoods in Buenos Aires.

Southwest

The southwestern border was no less complicated, but for completely different reasons than any other quadrant, with problems that are still alive today. Guano and nitrate mining began in the 1840s. Chile exploited these resources more quickly than Bolivia, resulting in the War of the Pacific and the loss of Bolivia's Pacific coast.

Once again, Spanish colonial maps were vague about borders between Bolivia, Peru, and Chile. From time to time, Chile and Bolivia agreed on which river or line of latitude should be the boundary, but the discovery of rich fields of guano, at first, followed by nitrates, changed all that.

Guano deposits were created over millions of years as rich, cold Pacific currents upwelled from the Antarctic, where the quantity of plankton supported large fish populations. Birds fed on the sea life for eons and there was no rainfall to wash away their droppings. The extremely arid Atacama desert was inhospitable to predators who would have culled the sea birds, so the birds' waste accumulated to layers up to sixty feet thick. The value of guano as fertilizer was known to the Inca, who protected the birds from hunting. The German explorer Alexander von Humboldt brought guano back to Europe and the British began to mine it by 1840, with Chilean and Chinese labor.

Bird droppings became big business, providing up to three-quarters of Peru's exports and were, for a time, South America's largest export. Three hundred Peruvian boats were involved in guano transportation. Guano was such a source of wealth that Spain, which lost its South American empire twenty-five years earlier, tried to get into the act too, sending warships to three small Peruvian islands. This act rallied all Andean countries to preserve their hard-won independence, especially Chile, which chased off the Spanish ships. The guano boom lasted thirty years, from 1840 to 1870.

In 1870, nitrates replaced guano as an even richer source of nitrogen for fertilizer, explosives, and industrial processes. Unlike the coastal guano deposits, the nitrates were inland, caused by millions of years of water washing down from the Andes and evaporating in the arid Atacama. Bolivia got its first railroads, built with Chilean capital, because the nitrate deposits required transportation to the coast. Whole towns were built, with housing, offices, and factories, whose empty ruins today make a jaw-dropping visit.

British money and Chilean workers developed the nitrate industry because Bolivian capital remained focused on the traditional highland mines, not on the coast. Chilean claims progressed farther and farther north. A three-way war ensued, with Peru and Bolivia pitted together against Chile. Bolivia's armies were easily defeated and left the field to Peru, who struggled on for three more years until Chilean troops ended up occupying Lima. It took until 1904 for Chile to make a final treaty with Bolivia. The treaty took all of the coastal lands, but as compensation for making Bolivia landlocked, Chile agreed to build a railroad from the Pacific to La Paz. Oddly, the railroad ended up partly in Peruvian territory. Fifer writes: "A Chilean railroad, built for Bolivia, in Peruvian territory, by a British company." The railroad began at Arica, a port that Peru built for Bolivia. It will never leave the Bolivian national consciousness that Arica should belong to Bolivia, even though it never has.

Thus, the saga of Bolivia's southwest border is a live issue today and promises to continue into the foreseeable future. The present form of the problem has to do with Bolivia exporting natural gas. Huge fields of gas have been discovered in southeastern and southern Bolivia and it would certainly be cheaper to export it through Chile. For all of its natural resources of agriculture, forests, fish, and minerals, Chile lacks energy. It would be natural for Bolivia to sell gas to Chile through the cheapest possible route, especially since Bolivia's biggest customer, Brazil, is discovering deposits of its own. However, in the early 2000s, when Bolivian president Goni Sánchez de Lozada wanted to make such a deal, Bolivia erupted with street demonstrations, road blockades, and strikes. Chile has repeatedly offered a duty-free corridor and five miles of coastline on which Bolivia could build a port, or use one of the existing Chilean ports, but Bolivia won't be satisfied until Chile returns sovereign territory on the Pacific.

Northwest

Lastly, the northwest quadrant provides yet another set of reasons why Bolivia's borders have been so much of a problem. No sooner had Bolivia become independent in 1825 than the country started making claims for Peruvian territory to link La Paz with Arica. Peru never had any advantage in giving over territory for a Bolivian corridor to the Pacific in the north. It would have split Peru into two parts, dividing the country from its Atacama lands, so Peru repeatedly ignored Bolivian offers.

The third Bolivian president, Andrés de Santa Cruz, saw Peru and Bolivia as being a natural single state. He invaded Peru and defeated its armies in one of the few post-independence battles that Bolivian armies ever won. But Chile saw a united Peru and Bolivia as being too strong a threat, so helped Peru, putting Chilean troops on the field disguised as Peruvians and eventually sending an army to defeat Santa Cruz near La Paz. Thus, Peru was in no mood to give Bolivia sovereign access to Arica.

The border around Lake Titicaca was yet another problem, but this was the only one settled amicably. Aymara and Quechua groups of both Peruvian and Bolivian affiliation were interwoven with considerable geographic complexity, so the nationality of the hacienda *patrón* was used to delimit the Bolivia-Peru border. Ninety-nine years of diplomatic negotiations, between 1842 and 1941, finally settled the border question peacefully. Fifer writes:

> The intricacies of this boundary when followed in the field, and knowledgeable detail incorporated into the terms of its delimitation are unique in the whole history of Bolivian boundary record. It is doubly unique in respect of the high density of population through which it passes, for nowhere else does Bolivia's perimeter pick its way so carefully through closely settled country, peopled well in advance of the international political divides of the nineteenth and twentieth centuries.

The Titicaca border with Peru is Bolivia's most successful border resolution.

North of Lake Titicaca in the lowlands, the border with Peru also took a long time to establish. The region was so remote as to be functionally not a part of the Spanish empire. Fortunately, the explorations of Colonel Pando in the 1890s helped establish the area as Bolivian, and the northern department is named after him. Peru also claimed vast tracts of this virtually uninhabited forest. Finds of quinine and rubber kept claims alive, coupled with stories of gold and land suitable for coffee.

Argentina was asked to arbitrate claims. After seven years of studying old maps, ordinances, and patents, and trying to factor in vague Spanish boundaries, a border commission compromised and suggested a border. Bolivians were unhappy with the choice. Mobs attacked the Argentine delegation in La Paz. Finally, the Brazilian government suggested a border adjustment in 1909, establishing what today is the straight part of the border, and the Royal Geographical Society in London was asked to demarcate it. After getting the rubber barons' private armies to stop sniping at each other, the Society cut a wide swath through the forest. Wooden pillars they erected were routinely overgrown within a year, but ultimately, the decline of the rubber industry extinguished the flames that fueled the dispute.

The very creation of Bolivia was contentious. Its size, shape, and rationale were precarious for a hundred years after independence. This absence of a strong *raison d'etre* was to cause every single border to be controversial. One result of this unlikely fusion of disparate lands into one country is that Bolivia encompasses an extensive diversity of people.

Demography

The North American concepts of race and ethnicity do not apply in Bolivia.

Consider twin brothers: if one lives in the city, wears western dress, has a job in the formal economy, and speaks Spanish, Bolivians would say he is a mestizo, (a mix of indigenous and European). If his twin brother remains in the countryside, wearing traditional dress, working at subsistence farming, and speaking only an indigenous language, Bolivians would say he is a *campesino*, a campo word (countryside), a more respectful term than "Indian" in 1952 after Victor Paz Estenssoro's national revolution. It would not matter if the parents of these twins were both pure-blooded indigenous people or if their heritage were mixed. It is the combination of language, employment, urban/rural location, and culture that determines whether a person is mestizo or *campesino*.

Bolivians use other names for indigenous people. *Cholas*, or a related term with a bit of endearment, *Cholitas*, are native women who dress in traditional highland style. This includes several wide skirts layered over one another, an English-style bowler hat, and tiny shoes that are patterned after those of Spanish bullfighters. They often carry a huge, multicolored sack on their backs, for they are typically traders. The husband of a *Chola* may be called a *Cholo*, but would more usually be called a *campesino* or *Indio*. The term *Indio*, depending on context and tone, may or may not be derogatory.

The Bolivian census does not gather data on what North Americans would call race or ethnicity. Instead, the Bolivian National Statistics Institute (*Instituto Nacional Estadística*) records language spoken at home. On that basis, the demography of Bolivia is 50% indigenous. To impose concepts of race and ethnicity beyond that, the other 50% are probably 35% mestizo and 15% white. It is important to know that Bolivia (and Guatemala) have the highest percentage of indigenous population in all of Latin America. Of Bolivia's native population, half are Quechua and one-third Aymara. Two small highland groups remain in the southern *altiplano*, but the remaining native groups, some thirty of them, are smaller tribes who live in the eastern lowlands and whose cultural identity is declining as more and more become mestizos. The population of Bolivia is about nine million, in about 35 different cultural groups.

These groups include Mennonites and Japanese. The Mennonites were invited by the governments of Bolivia and Paraguay in the 1950s to settle the sparse Chaco, so that each country could better claim ownership of disputed land. Some Mennonites live quite separate lives from other Bolivians, staying in their own towns and often not even learning Spanish. Other Mennonites have chosen to integrate. Many Japanese came to Bolivia after WWII when overpopulated Japan faced terrible food shortages. The Bolivian government provided land and the Americans gave farm implements to each Japanese family. Today, two Japanese communities exist north of Santa Cruz, Okinawa I and II. Older Japanese still live a traditional life, eating Japanese food and speaking Japanese, while many of their sons and daughters have moved to Brazil or integrated into Bolivian society.

Afro-Bolivians have a small but interesting presence. Brought by the Spanish as slaves to work in the mines of Potosí, many Africans suffered and died from inhumane working conditions and elevations of 14,000 ft (4,300 m). Some became domestic servants and others worked minting silver. When Potosí experienced one of its periodic mining busts, most Africans left for the

Norberto Ortega, in Sucre

more temperate lands of the Yungas, the transition zone in central
Bolivia between highlands and lowlands. One, Sambo Sambito,
became a Robin Hood above La Paz, robbing gold caravans from
the Yungas and distributing the money to the poor. Today, the
Afro-Bolivian community, about one percent of Bolivia's population, still lives in the Yungas where they are undergoing a cultural

Santos Domingo, in Potosí

revival, electing a king as leader and organizing international tours of music and dance.

Demography has a strong influence on current-day political problems. Ecuador, Peru, and Bolivia all have active indigenous-rights movements. In Bolivia, traditional political power lay in the *rosca*, a word for a rolled-up ball of string that in this case means the old-boy network of landowners and white, Spanish-descended elite. From the 1530s when the Spanish arrived in Bolivia, until 1952, indigenous groups were enslaved and their lands taken. Now, there is a backlash against that traditional political power structure. Indigenous groups have formed strong unions of miners, coca growers, teachers, transportation workers, and almost all sectors of employment. The most militant groups blockade roads with rocks or burning tires. There are frequent clashes with police.

The indigenous-rights movement rose to a new dimension when Bolivia freely elected Evo Morales as president in 2005, along with his political party, the Movement to Socialism. Born to a Quechua mother and an Aymara father, the first full-blooded indigenous president in Latin America, Morales was the head of the coca-growers union and had called for many road blockades and protests. Morales nationalized majority ownership of gas and oil, is friendly with Venezuela's Hugo Chávez, and is moving to change Bolivia's constitution with new election rules. Morales supports primary school education in native languages and removal of Catholicism as the required state religion taught in public schools. He lives modestly and cut his own salary by 47% (many Bolivian dignitaries and ambassadors earn vast amounts of money). Morales struggles with movements toward regional autonomy in the east and south, arguing that they are members of the *rosca* and seek wealth at the expense of the national good. Other challenges for any Bolivian president are formidable: poverty, labor unrest, building roads, and improving health and education.

Two

PRE-INDEPENDENCE HISTORY:
CIVILIZATIONS DESTROYED

Two quite separate early civilizations occupied Bolivia. The better known of the two is the Inca who evolved from a sequence of highland cultures that date from misty human origins on the continent. The lesser known is still unnamed, whose remains are to be found in the eastern lowlands. It is important to understand this history before Europeans, especially for the highland groups, both for its own sake and because the effects of this history are very much alive today.

Highlands

One must imagine early civilizations apart from the boundaries of modern-day Bolivia, which was not created until 1825. Prior to that time, groups were differentiated by language and cultures. Their boundaries overlapped with today's Bolivia and neighboring countries, especially Peru. For example, the first great, lasting civilization in Bolivia itself was Tiwanaku, but its existence depended on prior agriculture and social organization developed in the coastal regions and the *altiplano* north of Lake Titicaca.

The first humans in the Andes most likely arrived by water along the west coast of North and South America some 10,000 years ago, although recent archeological evidence in Chile could set the date back earlier. In any case, these early hunter-gatherer societies evolved into settled agricultural communities by 2500

Andean cross

BCE, forming an early phase of human development in the Andes. As food production was domesticated, the population grew and more complex forms of society developed, resulting in an archeological record today that includes towns and irrigation canals. Coastal areas were more developed, having been the site of man's arrival and lying in more moderate climates.

A second phase of Andean development dates from about 1200 BCE, marked by widespread pottery and advances in metallurgy. This early highland civilization is known as Wankarani, and whose remnants near Lake Poopó include carved stone or clay llama heads and evidence of copper smelting.

The most developed early highland civilization is called Chavín, whose people lived in central Peru from about 800–100

BCE. They are known for elaborate temples, stone monuments, and carved stonework of felines, birds, monkeys, and snakes. They engineered acoustical properties into temple rooms so that water flushed through conduits produced a roaring sound in the chambers. Walls were adorned by warriors with decapitated heads at their feet. One stone figure with jumbled eyes and jagged teeth holds a hallucinogenic cactus. Chavín people wove elaborate textiles and fashioned gold ornaments. While Chavín civilization did not reach south to Bolivia, it did influence, and was influenced by, coexistent groups called Chiripa and Pukara, peoples who lived on the shores of Lake Titicaca.

Unlike the scattered houses of the Wankarani, the Chiripa developed an urban structure. Stone masonry, carvings, and temples were later remodeled by the Tiwanaku people. The Chiripan archeological record reveals totora reeds, still used to build boats and the remarkable floating mats and villages that tourists see today near Puno, in Peru. Elaborate stone icons show a large human face surrounded by llamas and snakes, and they originated the "door-within-a-door," later adapted at Tiwanaku. Chiripa carvings include the Andean cross, whose top represents the heavens, symbolized by the condor, and whose right and left corners signify this world, symbolized by the puma and the llama. Below is the underworld, represented by a snake. Much of their architecture and stonework was adopted by Bolivian Tiwanakans.

Pukara culture flourished at a similar time as the Chavín and Chiripa, but is distinguished by its location on the northern shore of Lake Titicaca, while the Chiripa lived on the southern shore and Chavín in the northern *altiplano* of Peru. The archeological record of the Pukara shows extensive residential structures, temples, and fine ceramics, and the Pukara are also known for their agricultural terraces, ridged fields, water-collecting ponds, and canals. Visitors today can see the extensive remains of the Pukara around a town in Peru of the same name and the adoption of their agricultural constructions around Tiwanaku.

Reed boat made of totora reeds

Lowlands

Much less known are the ancient civilizations of the eastern lowlands. Someday in the future archeologists will piece together the components of this great, almost-lost nation. Perhaps they will find that many of the thirty-odd lowland groups descended from these ancient civilizations.

Ancient people inhabited the eastern lowlands northeast of Trinidad. A large and as yet unnamed civilization left a perplexing archeological record, consisting of large mounds, canals, roads, and vast quantities of ceramics. The culture originated some 3,000-

5,000 years ago and declined only 300-600 years ago. Descendants include a group called Baure, a people whose numbers are dwindling and whose language is disappearing. Most of the ruins are in the remote northeast department of Beni, but some are more accessible at Ibibaté, about 30 miles (50 km) east of Trinidad. There, 60 foot (18 m) high pyramids jut from the forest. Built largely of broken ceramics, these terraced mounds were surrounded by raised fields, in parallel or zig-zagged patterns, and connected by raised roads.

The roads are straight for several miles, often converging at low angles, almost parallel. Canals were dug beside them. Archeologists believe that the raised fields between the roads supported crops of beans, potatoes, manioc, and squash and that tree crops produced nuts and fruits. Baure people today prefer transporting goods by canoe rather than walking long distances on the roads. So, while the roads and canals most likely did serve a transportation function, and could have managed fish and floodwaters, their full use and reasons for construction are not well understood. Serious study of the archeological record did not begin until the late 20th century.

Human Ecology of the Altiplano

The separation of highland civilizations from eastern lowlands was quite complete. Methods of highland agriculture did not work in wet, hot lands, and the social organization it required was not present in the east. Diseases in the humid east were foreign to highlanders from dry climates. Even today, highlanders are bothered by the insects and suffer in the humidity of the lowland Amazon climate. However, highland civilizations were intimately connected with the *western* lowlands along the Pacific coast.

Within the *altiplano*, human ecology was founded on both crops and animals. In the arid high plains, people cultivated potatoes, *quinoa*, and legumes. The grazing of domesticated camelids (llamas and alpacas) provided meat, hides, wool, and fertilizer, while the undomesticated camelids (guanacos and vicuñas) were hunted.

The highlands were well connected to surrounding ecological zones. Highlanders traded their crops and animal products for fruits and dried fish with the western Pacific lowlands. Highland people ate maize and beans from the sub-*altiplano* valleys to the east (especially around Cochabamba). Coca leaf, used for medicine, as a stimulant, and in rituals, came from the Yungas (the transition zone between the *altiplano* and the eastern lowlands which lies northeast of La Paz). Because all of these different products were produced at different elevations, the trade is known among anthropologists as "verticality." Verticality increases nutrition and distributes risk, since highland area crops can be ruined by hail, rain, or drought.

Highland settlement was largely on the eastern side of the *altiplano*, the western side being too arid and largely devoid of the metals used by pre-Colombian highlanders, including gold, silver, tin, and copper. The population distribution today still reflects this human ecology.

Tiwanaku

Details of the archeological record are murky, although it is clear that by the beginning of the Christian era, a great settlement was present at Tiwanaku on the southern shores of Lake Titicaca. The lake, whose name probably means puma, provided a locally humid environment. Its waters moderated the cold and provided transportation. Huge temples were built of carefully hewn stone. Tall stones were erected whose positions tracked the sun and stars. Tiwanakan civilization supported a large population with irrigation canals and elevated crop beds that are still in use today.

Tiwanakans inherited much of their civilization from the Chavín, Chiripa, and Pukara, but contributed to Andean development through the building of fortified towns, the development of bronze (a mixture of tin and copper), and by extending their empire. Pottery and burial artifacts from Tiwanaku indicate that their culture stretched from Peru to Cochabamba, Arica, and San Pedro de Atacama in Chile. Long trains of llamas transported salt,

Lake Titicaca

textiles, maize, and metals. Tiwanakan culture also included "metaled" roads (stones held together with bronze links), irrigation, and intensification of agriculture. Skulls at Tiwanaku exhibit trepanation, which is surgery on the skull. Headless bodies were buried, hearkening back to the Chavín, suggesting that the carved stone heads in the subterranean court at Tiwanaku are the trophies of slain foes, although it is generally thought by anthropologists that most Tiwanakan expansion was peaceful. Tiwanakan culture formed at the southern end of Lake Titicaca.

Tiwanakan civilization lasted well over a thousand years, from about 100 BCE until 1200 CE. Why the culture collapsed is hazy. Its importance extends far beyond its demise, for the Tiwanakan people evolved into the modern Aymara, one of the two principal indigenous groups in Bolivia (along with Quechua, the descendants of the Inca).

The Aymara after Tiwanaku

After the fall of the Tiwanaku society, the Aymara divided into several groups, stretching from the Cuzco area to what is now southern Bolivia. Collectively, their reach extended far beyond that too, because each had colonies on the Pacific coast and in the eastern valleys like Cochabamba and the Yungas, exhibiting the verticality of earlier civilizations. The core area of the Aymara kingdoms surrounded Lake Titicaca. The Aymara fortified their towns, for the kingdoms fought among one another. The boundaries of a group's power were localized and are exhibited by *chulpas*, which are round or square towers made of stone or adobe that contain the burial remains of local leaders. These *chulpas* are visible today, scattered around the Andes from Puno to Oruro.

The Aymara dominated two other earlier groups, the Uru and Pukina. The Uru were probably focused around Lake Poopó. They apparently called their land Uru-Uru, which the Spanish came to pronounce as Oruro, giving the name to the sixth largest city in Bolivia. The Uru and Pukina were large groups—Pukina was the third-largest language of the *altiplano* by the arrival of the Spanish. Both groups were poor and subjugated by the Aymara.

The division of the Aymara into several groups led to internal weakness and their inability to defend themselves against a small but powerful group to the north, the Inca. The strongest and most well known Aymara kingdoms were the Lupaca and Colla. Each asked for an alliance with the Inca. When it was given to the Lupaca, the Colla attacked and was defeated. By the 1460s, the Inca took all of the Aymara Kingdoms.

Inca

There are several reasons why the Inca are the best known civilization of the Andes. One is that they were the dominant empire present upon the arrival of the Spanish. No Andean civilization had a written language, but early Spaniards did pass down knowledge of the Inca, so the record of evidence is simply more recent and better recorded.

Another reason is that the Incan Empire was so expansive. While the ethnic Inca numbered only 40,000, they ruled over several million, stretching from Colombia to central Chile. The Incan Empire lasted only a hundred years before being destroyed by the Spanish, even though it was highly organized and left behind roads and buildings.

The Inca also dominate the narratives of Spanish chroniclers and by extension Andean history because the Spanish, not knowing any better, believed and perpetuated the Inca's oral accounts of other peoples. The chronicler Garcilaso Inca de la Vega reveals the Incan bias when he quotes an old Incan general:

> ...at one time, all the land you see about you was nothing but mountains and desolate cliffs. The people lived like wild beasts, with neither order nor religion, neither villages nor houses, neither fields nor clothing, for they had no knowledge of either wool or cotton. Brought together haphazardly in groups of two and three, they lived in grottoes and caves and, like the wild game, fed upon grass and roots, wild fruits, and even human flesh. They covered their nakedness with the bark and leaves of trees, or with the skins of animals. Some of them even went unclothed. And as for women, they possessed none who were recognized as their very own.

This Inca distain led them to actively repress earlier civilizations. For example, their story of creation is that the Incan god Viracocha fashioned people out of mud on the shores of Lake Titicaca, as if no one had ever come before. Incan cosmology says that the great monuments of Tiwanaku were built by giants, not men.

Incan ruins on the Isla del Sol, Titicaca Lake, Bolivia. Image © Totorean

The very names "Inca" and "Quechua" are also misunderstandings by the Spanish. "Inca" meant a ruler, but came to be applied to their people and culture. "Quechua" were a tribe near Cuzco that the Inca conquered, and probably a Spanish misunderstanding applied the term to the Incan language (which the Inca called *Runa Simi*, or the language of people).

Despite their self-promotion, little was new with the Inca. Roads, irrigation, techniques of stone cutting and building, the structure of social organization, and extensive trade networks between highlands and lowlands all existed before them. What was improved by the Inca was a greater social organization that included a national tax system, unification and improvement of roads and communications, extensive warehousing and distribution of food, and common rule over a very large area.

The income for the Incan Empire was based on taxation of three things: agricultural products, labor, and textiles. To set the appropriate taxation of agricultural goods, land was divided into three categories of equal size. One was for the gods, which included priests and expenses for shrines and festivities of ancestor worship. The second was for the Incan emperor and the third for those tilling the land. The Inca depended heavily on a previously invented but modified system of labor taxation called *mita*, wherein villagers labored to build roads, temples, mines, irrigation, or serve in the army. Those laboring during their obligatory *mita* period of a few months were fed from the widespread food warehouses whose ruins still remain today. The third form of Incan taxation was of textiles, for cloth was of great importance, as it is among the indigenous in Bolivia today. Men made ropes for bridges, and women wove. Their designs even today identify their ethnic origin. Bird feathers were greatly prized, and the quality of clothing showed one's status.

There was no private property under the Inca, although careful property records were made, along with accurate tax records and censuses of people, all of which were kept on knotted ropes. Native social organization was left intact if a subjugated people did not resist. The Inca used pre-existing political structures, but re-educated the children of oppressed nobles by sending them to Cuzco to learn the language and the ways of the Inca. Incan state religion subsumed local beliefs under the Inca hierarchy, giving native peoples less reason to resist. Simple morals ruled, whose dictums today survive in song lyrics: do not lie, do not cheat, do not steal.

Inca road on Isla del Sol

The Spanish Conquest

The Spanish arrived in coastal Peru in 1528. As Francisco Pizarro and his financial backer, Diego de Almagro, sailed down the west coast of Peru, they saw large balsa trading rafts laden with vegetables, shells, and gold. Natives pointed out the Incan port of Tumbes as their home. The Inca gave the Spaniards a warm welcome, offering food and shelter among the fine buildings and well organized city. The gold on the temple walls greatly excited the Spanish. Pizarro and Almagro returned to Spain and showed the king Andean riches of gold, silver, and elaborate cloth. The king responded by giving Pizarro a license to explore and govern Peru. (Bolivia at that time was called Upper Peru because of the elevation.) Pizarro and Almagro returned to Peru with Pizarro's half-brothers Hernando, Juan, and Gonzalo.

The character of these men was coarse and brutal. They grew up in the Spanish backwater of Extremadura, a region of poverty that provided generations of soldiers for war against the Moors. Being a soldier was the only way to a better life. Treasure brought by Hernán Cortéz from Mexico fueled their dreams of conquest and riches from plunder. The great Incan Empire would be destroyed by illiterate, low-class opportunists, steeped in a cruel and violent history.

How could Pizarro and his 180 men and 27 horses destroy this empire of millions within a year of his arrival in 1532? One of the factors was smallpox and other European diseases. Others were the internal divisions of the Incan Empire and the power of Spanish horses and weaponry.

Smallpox arrived in the Caribbean in 1518, Mexico in 1520, and a mere eight years later in 1528, transmitted by human breath, it had worked its way down to the Andes, assisted by the efficient system of royal runners carrying messages thousands of miles throughout the Inca empire. Smallpox arrived just before Pizarro. The mortality estimate of an unvaccinated population without immunity is two thirds. In writer and filmmaker Michael Wood's fine book on the conquistadors, he points out that "…the disaster is psychological and social, as well as physical—a blow of fate so implacable and inexplicable that, in the short term, people lose the will to rebuild. 'Many died from hunger for they had no one left to look after them,' said the Aztecs in Mexico. 'No one cared about anyone else.'" In the Ecuadorian city of Cuenca, then called Tumi Bamba, the last Incan emperor, Wayna Capac caught the disease and swiftly died.

As he died, Wayna Capac's council of wise men asked him to name a successor. Some say he was so debilitated by the disease that he was confused and named an infant. He apparently also named both Atahualpa and his half-brother, Huascar. Each of the sons made a bid for legitimacy, Atahualpa taking the northern part of the empire and Huascar the southern. War broke out between them, just in time for the arrival of Pizarro. Huascar supported Pizarro, hoping he would defeat his enemy brother, and Pizarro did kill Atahualpa but then made Huascar into a pawn. Thus, the weak and badly divided empire was easy prey for the Spaniards. Then of course, the Spanish had guns, mechanical crossbows, and steel armor. Their horses and dogs terrified indigenous people.

William Hickling Prescott, the great American historian of the Spanish conquest, wrote in the nineteenth century:

When Pizarro obtained possession of Cuzco, he found a country well advanced in the arts of civilization; institutions under which the people lived in tranquility and personal safety; the mountains and the uplands whitened with flocks; the valleys teeming with the fruits of a scientific husbandry; the granaries and warehouses filled to overflowing; the whole land rejoicing in its abundance; and the character of the nation, softened under the influence of the mildest and most innocent form of superstition, well prepared for the reception of a higher and a Christian civilization. But, far from introducing this, Pizarro delivered up the conquered races to his brutal soldiery; the sacred cloisters were abandoned to their lust; the towns and villages were given up to pillage; the wretched natives were parceled out like slaves, to toil for their conquerors in the mines; the flocks were scattered, and wantonly destroyed, the granaries were dissipated; the beautiful contrivances for the more perfect culture of the soil were suffered to fall into decay; the paradise was converted into a desert. Instead of profiting by the ancient forms of civilization, Pizarro preferred to efface every vestige of them from the land, and on their ruin to erect the institutions of his own country. Yet these institutions did little for the poor Indian, held in iron bondage. It was little to him that the shores of the Pacific were studded with rising communities and cities, the marts of a flourishing commerce. He had no share in the goodly heritage. He was an alien in the land of his fathers.

In the end, the greed of the Pizarro gang caused them to destroy themselves. Francisco Pizarro was killed in Lima by the son of Diego Almagro. Almagro himself, having conquered lands to the south in Chile and finding little of value, turned his army against Francisco Pizarro's brothers in Cuzco, Gonzalo and Fernando. Almagro was garroted and beheaded. Hernando Pizarro, the most educated of the brothers, returned to Spain and spent twenty years in prison for the misdeeds of his brothers. Gonzalo Pizarro, possibly the worst of the lot, led his army against a Spanish viceroy. His soldiers deserted him and he too was beheaded. Most of the vast wealth of silver in Bolivia was looted by foreigners and thriving civilizations were destroyed.

Indigenous rebellions did occur throughout colonial times— more than 100 revolts happened throughout the highlands of Bolivia in the 18th century alone. While most were local and uncoordinated, one rebellion in 1780–1782 involved 100,000 native people. It stretched from Cuzco through Upper Peru to Argentina and was led by an educated and literate man born as José Gabriel Condorcanqui who took his ancestor's name Túpac Amaru. He was killed in a siege of Cuzco, while the fight was carried on for another year by indigenous leaders and commoners. There is a long history of indigenous opposition to the institutions of colonialism that serves as backdrop for today's indigenous-rights movements.

Potosí

Perhaps no single place epitomizes the colonial period like the city and mines of Potosí, a must-see in Bolivia, for it was Potosí that financed the Spanish empire for a hundred years. Herbert Klein, who is widely respected in Bolivia as an authority on Bolivian history, writes: "During this period [1570–1650], Potosí alone produced over half of the silver of the New World and was unquestionably the world's single most important source of the mineral." The mines at Cerro Rico produced twenty billion ounces of silver. Klein explains that all of Europe became wealthier from increased trade with Asia because Europe was able to pay the Chinese in their preferred currency, silver.

In his book on Potosí, Stephen Ferry describes the city in the seventeenth century:

> [Potosí] had thirty-six magnificently decorated churches, thirty-six gambling houses, and fourteen dance academies. Salons, theaters, and fiesta stage-settings had the finest tapestries, curtains, heraldic emblazonry, and wrought gold and silver; multicolored damasks and cloths of gold and silver hung from the balconies of houses…The ladies sparkled with diamonds, rubies, and pearls; the gentlemen sported the finest embroidered fabrics from Holland. Bullfights were followed by tilting contests, and love and pride inspired frequent medieval-style duels with emerald-studded, gaudily plumed helmets, gold filigree saddles and stirrups, Toledo swords, and richly caparisoned Chilean ponies.

Klein describes how all of Bolivia and even Peru and Argentina were tied to Potosí. Mules and llamas transported all silver out and all goods in. Cochabamba and Tarija grew by producing wheat and corn, and Sucre flourished as Potosí's administrative capital. Mines in Peru produced mercury for the process of refining silver, and individuals in Lima amassed fortunes providing investment capital for Potosí. The Yungas east of La Paz boomed from rising demand for coca. The economic fortunes of Bolivia were intimately tied to Potosí.

Potosí today is the poorest department in the poorest country in South America. Embedded in songs and consciousness, many indigenous remember the fantastic wealth of silver that accrued to foreigners, leaving the indigenous in poverty, with low education levels, few job opportunities, and little health care. Much bitterness remains over these injustices of the past whose residual effects are still part of everyday life for many.

The Legacy of Colonialism

Spain ruled Bolivia from Pizarro's time until independence in 1825. This is not past history. The effects of colonialism are profound and include changing the control of land from indigenous to Spanish, commandeering indigenous labor, the replacement of native governance with European, and creation of a system of wealth and class segregation.

Modern post-colonial society stands in stark contrast to indigenous traditions of land and labor. Indigenous groups had elaborate systems of land management that were woven into the fabric of their societies. Consider the Aymara. Access to land was decided by a combination of small villages and kin groups who dictated that no one person controlled a large amount of land. The Aymara did not amass wealth in the hands of one person or a small group of people. If an individual did acquire more wealth than others, he would be asked to finance some of the many rituals that involved whole villages. He would be expected to serve in civil-religious offices and pay the expenses associated with them. In these ways, indigenous people distributed wealth. Herbert Klein calls this "ritual impoverization." Even today, a large landholder, native or otherwise, will be asked to finance local festivals. Labor was shared in similar ways and governed by the same structures. To prepare fields or at harvest, many laborers would come together for the long, arduous process. They would earn the right to have their fellows reciprocate.

While native people had elaborate systems to allocate land, the Spanish introduced the *encomienda* system that resulted in *haciendas*, huge swathes of land controlled by the few of Spanish descent, setting the foundation for the unequal distribution of wealth that exists today. The *encomienda* system was created by the Spanish crown to lower the expenses of maintaining colonies. An officer in the army, a civil administrator, or someone who upheld the crown's domain was rewarded with a grant of land and the labor of the people who lived on it. At first, *encomienda* grants were for one or two generations, with the rights to three months' labor of the people who lived there. However, by the 18th century, land was appropriated permanently as *haciendas* with all of the labor owing to the Spanish landowner. (Homesteads of *haciendas* are sometimes visible today by clumps of trees surrounding the site of the house, for it was not the custom of natives to plant trees.) Bolivian presidents throughout the early 19th century repeatedly appropriated "communal" native lands and reassigned them to the state. The state sold them to *blancos* and gave them to the church. The *blancos* then had a legal title on a registered piece of paper, but the indigenous had no such thing. *Blancos* could offer their land title as collateral, gaining access to bank loans as a pool of capital to finance a business, but this was not an option for indigenous people. Even today, clear land titles for indigenous people are a major issue in Bolivia.

Besides land appropriation, Spanish colonists broke up much of the native social organization and radically altered their labor. Viceroy Francisco Toledo in Lima reorganized indigenous communities, destroyed traditional land management, and resettled them in smaller towns, making more land available for colonists. While some labor was directly appropriated by the colonists, the imposition of a tax (payable in products or money) forced landless natives to become migrants in a monetary economy. Indigenous people were still paying 60% of government revenue in the 1820s.

It is more than an abstract exercise in history to understand how the colonial system impoverished natives, for any traveler in Bolivia today needs to be aware of the simmering discontent that can erupt on roads with burning tires and stones blocking traffic, of militant protests, and tear gas.

Many indigenous Bolivians believe that some form of native social organization should replace European-based politics that were designed to oppress them. This psychology underlies modern Andean movements for indigenous rights, a potent force in Bolivia today. Among Bolivia's neighbors, only Peru and Ecuador have a high proportion of native population—Bolivia is at 50%, Peru 45%, and Ecuador 25% (while Chile, Argentina, Paraguay, and Brazil have only 1–5%). The legacy of colonialism lives on in Bolivia today.

Bolivian women walking near Lake Titicaca. Image © Totorean

Three

POST-INDEPENDENCE HISTORY: CHAOTIC POLITICS

The character of Bolivia is strongly formed by its chaotic political history. The country has experienced extreme and frequent swings of government, lurching from dictator to dictator and from one economic policy to another.

The pandemonium that is Bolivian politics is an important reason why the country is poor. With over 200 coups and attempted coups since independence in 1825, a president lasts an average of ten months. One day in 1970 saw six presidents on the same day. Coherence and consistency of government policies is not possible in such a political environment. Key issues that run through 200 years of Bolivian politics and economics include: the role of the indigenous in politics, government or private control of natural resources, and socialism vs. market economics.

The Struggle for Independence: 1809–1825

The story of the fractious Bolivian politics of independence starts in Europe when Napoleon Bonaparte invaded Spain in 1807-08. He deposed the Spanish King Ferdinand VII and set up a French government, but soon Madrid rebelled. One result was fragmented loyalties in South America: some supported Ferdinand; others his sister Carlota, who was married to a Portuguese prince who ruled Brazil. The views of local governors in the Americas differed from royal officials there; and both conflicted with Creoles and mestizos who wanted local rule by citizens' councils. These factionalized groups played out their aspirations in a long series of wars that left newly independent Bolivia with burnt haciendas, destroyed mines, plundered cities, uncertain borders, and an empty mint.

The first spark of independence in Bolivia was provided by Pedro Domingo Murillo, a mestizo who declared independence in 1809 and established a short-lived citizens' council. Local Spanish Creole troops didn't want to kill their fellows to put down the insurrection, so the Viceroy in Lima sent 5,000 soldiers from Cuzco to pursue Murillo and his small band into the Yungas, where they captured him and then hung him in the main plaza in La Paz that bears his name today. Bolivia was the first South American country to declare independence and the last to get it.

Buenos Aires declared independence in 1810 and led repeated expeditions to free Upper Peru, most defeated by the cruel Spanish general Goyeneche. Bolivian cities either joined the Argentines or rebelled on their own. The most famous of those revolts was in Cochabamba in 1812, when the women of the city fought because their men were dead or fighting elsewhere. The event is enshrined as Mother's Day in Bolivia.

It took fifteen years of war to liberate Bolivia. Final success came from outside, from Venezuela's Simón Bolívar and Argentina's José de San Martín. Joined by local leaders and local armies, Bolívar's troops eventually defeated the factions caused by breakup in Spain. Rising young military stars who would become Bolivian presidents led their forces to victory over Spanish royalist forces at Junín and Zepita. Lima's Viceroy de la Serna lost the Battle of Ayacucho in 1824 and the generally pro-loyalist General Olañeta, who commanded a private independent army, was finally killed by his own men in 1825.

Bolívar opposed the very idea of Bolivia. He wanted a united South America, even though his advisors argued that a buffer state was needed between powerful Lima and Buenos Aires. Eventually,

Bolívar succumbed to regional pressures for independent states. After serving as temporary president for a few months in a country he didn't want but which was named after him anyway, Bolívar returned to Colombia and Venezuela where he died disillusioned as he waited for a ship to take him permanently to Europe.

Antonio de Sucre and Andrés Santa Cruz: 1825–1941

The legacy of war left the newborn country decimated. Mining was in decline because the source of investment capital, Lima, was now in another country, and transportation costs increased as Bolivia's traditional export routes through Peru now faced a Peruvian trade barrier. To make matters worse, silver production in Potosí dropped as labor costs rose because Bolívar had abolished the *mita* labor system, so the mines at Potosí no longer profited from free labor. Water filled the mines and the silver stored there was looted by the Argentines. Citizens turned to subsistence agriculture.

The first two lasting presidents of Bolivia were officers in Bolívar's army: José Antonio de Sucre and Andrés Santa Cruz. Both undertook wide-ranging reforms with varying degrees of success. Sucre weakened the power of *hacienda* owners by taxing them and confiscating their estates. He took power from the church by ending rents paid for church agricultural land. Monasteries and convents were reduced and their land and privileges taken away. He tried to reform the tax system by taxing land and urban property, though with a dormant economy he had no choice but to return to taxing indigenous people for the majority of state revenues. An assassination attempt and a failed coup led Sucre to resign power and return to his native Venezuela.

Bolivia's second president, Andrés Santa Cruz, instituted more reforms. He codified civil and commercial laws in a new constitution. He lowered mining taxes thereby broadening the source of revenue for the state, though he too relied heavily on taxing the indigenous. In these ways, Santa Cruz balanced the budget and made Bolivia debt-free. He opened the Universidad Mayor de San Andrés in his native La Paz. He built a road to the port city of

Cobija, since Peru heavily taxed goods in and out of Bolivia's natural ports at Lima and Arica. However, his downfall was that old fractious legacy before independence, for he took the opportunity of a civil war in Peru to invade and force a federation of the two countries. While his new state brought peace to Peru, the possibility of a powerful and united neighbor to the north caused Chile to invade Bolivia and defeat Santa Cruz. Santa Cruz was exiled to France, where he died a disillusioned man like both his predecessors. A local government official assumed power in La Paz in 1839 but within two years was overthrown by the first of Bolivia's *caudillos*.

Caudillos: 1841–1880

Bolivia entered a period of *caudillos* (strong men) from 1841–1880. Dictators were the norm, and even with an occasional election (four in that period), presidents turned despotic. Not only was society damaged by authoritarian rule, the state treasury was depleted over and over despite one of Bolivia's biggest silver booms. Steam power was implemented in the sliver mines to pump out water and increase production, so government coffers grew, but instead of government revenues being spent on infrastructure or education (literacy was seven percent), a bloated and officer-heavy army exhausted human and physical capital. The first *caudillo*, José Ballivián, though a military man himself, tried to decrease the size of the army, which consumed almost half of state revenues. Two dictators later, the military still used 41% of government funds.

Ballivián was followed by Manuel Isidoro Belzú. Herbert Klein writes: "Without an established political party system to channel demands or aspirations or control appetites, national politics was a gruesome free-for-all in which any small-time regional leader could play. The result was that Belzú had to face something on the order of thirty to forty different revolts in his six years in government." Although Belzú favored improving the situation of the indigenous and the lower classes, incessant infighting trumped any progress. Political chaos continued to thrive when Belzú was

Metal cross on red church in the city of Tupiza, Bolivia. Image © Elifranssens

followed by Linares and Achá. Achá is best known for massacring his political opposition— known as the "murders of Yáñez" after the general who executed 71 supporters of the rival Belzú.

The most infamous of the *caudillos* was Mariano Melgarejo. Not quite all of the stories about him are true, but most are. He did call out his troops in the middle of the night and began marching them to Europe to fight in the Franco-Prussian war. One account has him returning to Oruro because of a cold rain the following morning. Another describes the next day as they rode toward France, a bold general asked Melgarejo how he planned to provide transport across the ocean. "Ocean?" replied Melgarejo. "There is an ocean?"

Usually drunk, he once ordered his soldiers to march out of a second-story window to show a visiting foreign minister how disciplined and subordinate his army was. He did have his mistress dance naked on the tabletop during military meetings. If generals at the meeting "lost their composure," he had them shot. Melgarejo once said to a large crowd, "I have put the constitution of 1861, which was very good, in this pocket, and that of 1868, which is even better, in this one, and nobody is going to rule Bolivia but me."

Melgarejo tried to take indigenous land to replenish the state treasury he was busily draining. He declared that native communal lands belonged to the state and decreed that native people had sixty days in which to buy their lands or else they would be auctioned. Only whites and mestizos had money, and so began a land grab that resulted in loss of prime indigenous lands.

Melgarejo didn't stop there. He sold Bolivian land to Brazil, reputedly for a horse, then gave away sovereign Bolivian territory to Chile. He so readily relinquished land to Chile that it gave Chileans a taste for more, which they would soon get in the War of the Pacific that followed Melgarejo's rule. Chile was so pleased with Melgarejo that they gave him the position of honorary general in the Chilean army.

Brewing on Bolivia's coastline was the greatest territorial loss in the country's history. Centuries of bird droppings along the

Pacific coast from birds feeding on the cold, nutrient-rich waters from Antarctica, built up in layers tens of feet deep. With no natural predators in the Atacama Desert, the bird guano accumulated. High in nitrates, both the guano and the nitrates from lake evaporation were rich fertilizer and useful in industrial processes. Slowly, with British financing and Chilean labor, Chile mined farther and farther north while mining interests in Bolivia focused on the highlands. Little thought was given to developing coastal nitrates. When Hilarión Daza, Melgarejo's successor, instituted a tax on Chilean nitrate exports, Chile in 1879 invaded both the Bolivian coastal province of Antofagasta and the Peruvian province of Tarapaca. The bulk of fighting ended in 1880, with a partial treaty in 1884, but a final peace treaty was not signed until 1904.

The consequences of the War of the Pacific were far reaching. Bolivia lost its coastline and would use ocean access as an excuse for starting the Chaco War in the 1930s. A state treasury bulging from silver revenues was wasted. The loss of Bolivian pride is still evident today, with parades, signs, and speeches demanding the return of coastal land.

The only good to come from the War of the Pacific was that it stimulated fifty years of better government in Bolivia. The excesses of military dictatorships were so evident that civilian rule followed, with a modern parliamentary structure and formation of political parties.

Rosca Government, Silver, and Tin: 1880–1932

A rejuvenation of silver mining also stimulated better government as mine owners wanted both peace and railroads. Bolivian capital built the silver industry of the 1880s and '90s as the silver barons invested in electrification of the mines, enabling them to efficiently pump out water that flooded the lower levels and to mechanize ore removal. The mine owners exercised strong influence on government, three of them becoming presidents.

Hacienda owners played a similar role. Melgarejo's schemes worked to transfer "communal" lands from indigenous people to *blancos*. The indigenous did not participate in government because of a literacy requirement to vote. Thus, political power was bound up in what Bolivians even today call the *rosca*, a word for a being curled up in a ball, or in this case, an old-boys network. There were elections and coups during 1880-1930, but coups were accomplished with little violence, and power held by the mining and landed elite ensured continuity. Herbert Klein estimates that the Spanish-speaking population during this period was about a quarter, with 10–20% of the population participating in politics and government.

Silver mining declined steeply with a fall in world silver prices at the turn of the century, but Bolivia was fortunate to make an immediate transition to tin. Little changed in politics as tin barons replaced silver magnates, although a new political party was formed, the Liberals, who intensified the previous Conservative Party's efforts to seize indigenous lands. The tin barons, Simon Patiño, the Aramayo family, and Mauricio Hochschild, were all Bolivians (though Hochschild was European-born, he lived in Bolivia for much of his life). While the tin barons did not take the presidency, their surrogates did, so that the *rosca* continued, producing the most stable period in Bolivian history—no coup attempts for 21 years between 1899 and 1920 (a record broken only in 2003).

The 1920s and '30s saw the rise of labor unions, a potent force in Bolivian history and in today's politics. Begun in the mines, labor unions led miners to demonstrate for better working conditions. The army responded with a 1923 massacre of miners and their families in Uncía, where Simon Patiño built his tin empire. Two large indigenous uprisings were suppressed in the same way—one near Lake Titicaca and another at Potosí. A pattern was begun that would see the army massacre union strikers, a dynamic present in Bolivia until the 1980s. This frequent use of the army to suppress labor unrest is discernable today as various police forces are used against strikes instead of the army because of the army's reputation for vicious labor suppression.

Tin declined by the late 1920s as other areas of the world began to produce it and the price decreased. Bolivian tin was more expensive to transport to world markets because the country was not located near ocean shipping. It was more expensive to refine because its ores were generally of lower concentration. The world's economic depression of the 1930s further depressed Bolivia's economy.

The Chaco War: 1932–1935 and its Aftermath: 1936–1952

Declining government revenues and increasing labor protest set the stage for Bolivia's second disastrous war. With its main source of revenue drying up, the president elected in 1931, Daniel Salamanca, faced a catastrophe. Strikes increased and foreign debt could not be repaid. The new president met students and labor union strikes with even greater violence and fabricated a foreign devil in Standard Oil's development of oil fields in Santa Cruz.

Salamanca needed a scapegoat and found one in the Chaco War. Arguing to the nation that internal mine-union communists and radicals were a threat to the country's stability and that foreign corporations were building wealth at Bolivians' expense, Daniel Salamanca started the Chaco War. Using the excuse of Paraguayans' presence at an obscure lake in the arid Chaco in 1932, so remote that repeated patrols had to be sent even to find it, Salamanca whipped up national sentiment so that Bolivia would not lose land or access to the River Paraguay the way it did in the Atacama.

The Chaco itself had nothing worth fighting for. No minerals were known there, the few natives inhabiting the land were hostile, agriculture was not productive, and no matter what treaty was considered, Bolivia always had legal access to the River Paraguay with or without the Chaco War.

Bolivia had considerable military advantage at the start of the war. With a long tradition of military service, a military budget three times larger than Paraguay's, and far more military equipment, Bolivia would both start the Chaco War and lose it.

Bolivia did have a few military successes early in the war, until long supply lines and a determined Paraguayan army caused them to evaporate. The Bolivian army was directed by an old German officer, General Hans Kundt, who used World War I tactics against a more mobile army that repeatedly outflanked and surrounded Bolivian units. Bolivia instituted a military draft to supply soldiers. Indigenous men were drafted from their highland villages with no idea where the Chaco was or why there was a war. Many spoke only Quechua or Aymara, while their officers spoke only Spanish. Thousands of Bolivian soldiers died of thirst while an incompetent field supply chain failed to deliver water, food, bullets, and transport.

The Paraguayan field commander, Mariscal Estigarribia, boldly struck at Bolivian supply lines and used water sources to strategic advantage. Barefoot Paraguayan soldiers, who believed their country would be erased from the map unless they were victorious, fought effectively under their wily field commander. While political doubts translated into divisive military leadership on the Bolivian side, the Paraguayan effort enjoyed unified support and a single-minded national commitment.

Gradually, Paraguay pushed the Bolivians back, but Paraguay lost their advantage of knowing their local terrain as fighting entered the highlands of Bolivia, so that Bolivia once again won sporadic victories. The war ended in a stalemate in 1935. The new League of Nations, formed at the end of WWI to prevent international wars, was completely ineffective. Ninety thousand men were dead, the Bolivian economy even worse than before, and the borders remained effectively the same.

However, like the War of the Pacific, the disaster that was the Chaco War shook Bolivia into better government. While most of the Chaco War generals would become Bolivian presidents, public sentiment led them to address Bolivia's problems. Political parties were reformed and focused on social issues. The political agenda changed from mining and railroads to questions about land ownership and the status of indigenous Bolivians. These questions would drive Bolivia to its next great event, Victor Paz Estenssoro's revolution of 1952.

Post-Chaco War government saw the growth of national socialism under former war generals-turned-presidents: David Toro, Germán Busch, and Enrique Peñaranda. The state again became heavily involved in mining. Standard Oil's assets were nationalized as leaders demonized economic imperialism. Politics shifted strongly as three political parties formed to oppose the *rosca* oligarchy: a nationalist socialist party, the MNR (*Movimiento Nacionalista Revolucionario*); the leftist PIR (*Partido de la Izquierda Revolucionaria*) under university professor Antonio Arce, Marxist university students, and radical labor organizations; and the POR (*Partido Obrero Revolucionario*) of Trotskyites.

Politics became increasingly polarized as the oligarchy resurged even while leftist parties gathered strength. This palpable tension would be the backdrop for violence and tumult through the 1940s and leading to the 1952 revolution. The oligarchy employed the military to overthrow the government and when even the *rosca* lost control, they gave the government to the military. Peñaranda was one such vehicle of the *rosca*. He restored relations with the U.S. in the early years of WWII. The U.S. responded with five million dollars in loans, of which 1.75 million was compensation to Standard Oil for earlier nationalization of their assets. Documents that created the fiction of Nazi control over Bolivia were forged, probably by the British, and accepted by the U.S. The story was used to repress the MNR and close their newspaper. Peñaranda's government also repressed miners' strikes, notably Catavi in 1942. As miners and their families approached the Catavi headquarters to demand higher wages, the army laid in wait behind a shallow ridge. They fired most of the day at the miners, killing over 300 men, women, and children. Carried out by the PIR Minister of Labor, the army's massacre of miners in Catavi brought down Peñaranda.

The MNR came to power in a coup in 1943 under an unknown army officer, Gualberto Villarroel. While Villarroel's government finally saw the end of the *mita* system of indigenous labor, he became violently repressive of his political opposition,

La Paz at night, © *Javarman*

with his goons rounding up opposition leaders and pushing them off the high cliffs of the road between La Paz and Coroico. A monument on the road today gives the names of those killed. Their bodies were found days later as dogs from a nearby mining camp came back bloated and stinking. Sixty opposition members were murdered, leading the public to drag Villarroel from office and hang him from a light pole in Plaza Murillo.

The *rosca* returned in 1946 and governed until the 1952 revolution. Violence continued as the strongest of unions, the miners' union, gained momentum through the later 1940s. The philosophy of the Trotskyite miners' union is described by Bolivian historian Waltraud Queiser Morales: "The program's Trotskyist belief in permanent revolution stressed the necessity of the armed class struggle led by the workers—the only truly revolutionary class in Bolivia. Accommodation with democratic regimes was out of the question; the goal was an immediate socialist revolution and worker state. This program of violent class struggle was at odds with the multiclass strategy of the MNR and amounted to a declaration of war against the *rosca*." Teachers and postal workers struck. The MNR sponsored a revolution in 1949 but botched it with poor planning and bad luck. Victor Paz Estenssoro, whose MNR newspaper was closed by the Nazi fabrication, helped plan the 1949 revolution from exile in Argentina.

Paz Estenssoro's National Revolution: 1952–1964

Finally an election was held in 1951 that the MNR won overwhelmingly. The *rosca* handed the government to the military, who annulled the elections, and the spark for the 1952 revolution was struck. Victor Paz Estenssoro returned from exile in Argentina, and after a brief civil war leaving 500 dead, the revolution of 1952 was underway.

Paz Estenssoro was to become one of the most important political figures in Bolivian history, but his political orientation cannot be easily characterized because of an abrupt about-face in political and economic policies. The policies of Estenssoro ranged from initial Peronist-style populism styled after Argentina to later pro-U.S. and conservative IMF economic policies.

Estenssoro's MNR immediately enacted profound reforms. The right to vote was extended to everyone. Prior to 1952, only the literate could vote, and practically speaking, this meant that only a small percent of the population voted. The big tin mines were nationalized under COMIBOL (the *Corporación Minera de Bolivia*) and the government immediately controlled almost all foreign exports and half of government revenues. Land laws gave natives access to land and abolished their debt servitude. This access to land can hardly be overemphasized in a country where 72% of the population was engaged in agriculture and 80% was rural. Prior to 1952, 6% of the population owned 92% of land. Agricultural extension and rural development were planned to improve the lives of the indigenous (though little was actually done). Education was provided for all. The MNR decimated the army and police and distributed arms to the masses (soon to be taken back).

Then the economy crashed. Spending on the mines and social programs drained government income. Land policies resulted in less food to cities, so massive food imports began. The government printed money and inflation rates soared over 900%. The middle class abandoned the MNR as urban property valued dropped. Miners received housing and equipment almost for free. They responded by buying as much as they could from the government and reselling it in a thriving black market.

It was time for Paz Estenssoro's about-face. Much of the MNR's government largesse for social programs was funded by U.S. assistance, conditional on a more moderate revolutionary stance, and most of the oil production around Santa Cruz was developed with U.S. investment. U.S. aid funded education, road building, health, and food. Though the U.S. would have preferred not to fund such a left-leaning government, Washington feared that Bolivia would slip into communist hands if they didn't. Paz Estenssoro acquiesced. He compensated the tin barons. He reformed Bolivia's economic policies to be IMF-compliant, cutting government spending, constricting the money supply, and resuming debt payments. Food subsidies decreased, wages were lowered, and the country was required to balance its budget. He de-nationalized oil and allowed U.S. companies to control Bolivian resources.

Military Governments: 1964–1982

Paz Estenssoro played the moderate between left and right factions of the MNR. Under U.S. influence, the leftist elements of the MNR were suppressed. The conservative economic policies were working. Paz was elected to a second term, and carried on his pro-army, anti-labor and even more markedly pro-U.S. policies. Paz served a second term but as he approached a third, the polarized MNR party factions of left and right prevented him from fostering one of the two leading MNR candidates, as had been previously agreed. Instead, Paz was elected to a third term with his vice-president René Barrientos. A few months after the 1964 election Barrientos and the army overthrew Paz in a bloodless coup, initiating two decades of military power in Bolivia.

Barrientos continued the later-phase MNR policies of IMF compliance, union opposition, and pro-U.S. policies. He was particularly repressive of miners and their union, the FSTMB, and the general labor union, the COB (*Federación Sindical de Trabajadores Mineros de Bolivia* and the *Central Obrera Boliviana*). Barrientos fired all miners in the FSTMB. He took COB control of the government-owned mining corporation COMIBOL and turned it over to a military general. He reduced the size of the COMIBOL bureaucracy and its number of miners. Worst of all, he ordered the army to violently repress miners, culminating in more army massacres at the Catavi and Siglo XX mines in 1967. His pro-U.S. policies included giving U.S. oil companies rights to produce and export oil and gas, and he gave the U.S. intelligence about Ché Guevara, which led to the 1967 killing of the Cuban revolutionary in the remote hills southwest of Santa Cruz. Barrientos governed until 1969 when he was killed in a helicopter crash.

The military dictators who followed Barrientos for two years swung Bolivia far to the left. The first of them renationalized oil companies and reinstated the unions. The second, Juan José Torres, turned against the U.S., accepting Russian aid and throwing the Peace Corps out of Bolivia. The day of Torres's coup was the day when Bolivia had six presidents all on the same day (4 October 1970).

With conservative businessmen estranged and the military alienated by Torres's military spending cut and his tolerance of civilian influence in military matters, it was time for another coup.

The coup in 1971 brought Colonel Hugo Banzer to power. Banzer was to become another important figure in Bolivian politics in the latter half of the twentieth century. He ruled Bolivia as a dictator from 1971–78 and as an elected president from 1997-2002. Banzer represented a military government that supported business interests and repressed labor unions. Supported by the middle and upper classes, Banzer again allied Bolivia with the U.S., welcoming foreign investors in resource extraction, and accepting both large foreign loans and military assistance. Even though wages were frozen, prices fluctuated freely. Elected union officials were replaced by government officials. Workers became increasingly angry, blocking roads and hosting demonstrations. A hundred peasants were killed near Cochabamba in the massacre of Tolata in 1974. With violent army action against peasants protesting food prices, unsanctioned strikes and demonstrations, and a hunger strike in the cathedral in La Paz, U.S. President Jimmy Carter's pro human-rights policies reduced support for Banzer and he was overthrown by the military. The two years following Banzer, from 1978–80, saw several more coups and military governments, plus two elected leaders that briefly included Bolivia's only female president, Lidia Gueiler Tejada. During her short presidency, Gueiler decided to remove army commander Luis Garcia Meza from power, prompting him to stage a coup and rule from 1980–81.

Garcia Meza became the country's worst modern president, leading a government called the "cocaine mafia." Meza appointed a drug trader as the national counternarcotics police chief. The Minister of the Interior was also a drug lord, who taxed every bale of coca at forty dollars and kept ten for himself. Meza invited the Argentine military to teach the Bolivians how to conduct disappearances of human rights leaders. The church and foreign journalists were muzzled. Army officers seized their chance to make a fortune smuggling gems and drugs. Photos of Meza and his cronies show them grinning defiantly from under tall military hats.

Meza reserved his most bitter vehemence for striking miners. At Caracoles and Viloco, Meza's drunken troops committed one of the worst massacres in Bolivian history. Miners were executed with dynamite, women raped and killed, and children were made to eat gunpowder, after which soldiers laid them on broken glass and walked on them. At the big mines of Huanuni, Catavi, and Siglo XX, the brutality was so bad that conscripted soldiers refused to butcher their fellow countrymen, so officers shot their soldiers instead.

One of Meza's cronies was the Nazi Butcher of Lyon, Klaus Barbie, who as a Gestapo officer killed 4,000 people in concentration camps during WWII. Barbie came to Bolivia in 1951 and took a job in the Yungas as manager of a sawmill for a Jew, Ludwig Kapauner. Early in his employment, Kapauner returned from a business trip and noticed that some of his trees had been defaced by swastikas. Barbie promptly organized a work party of laborers to scrape off the offensive symbols. Barbie made some money in the sawmill business, exported quinine to Vietnam during the Vietnam War, and started a shipping business in La Paz. The president of Bolivia invited him to buy and manage ships that were supposed to become the merchant marine of Bolivia, but Barbie never bought the ships. He used the money to rent some instead. Everyone thought Bolivia had a merchant marine, but Barbie used the ships for his own gun-running business. In perhaps his most bizarre business deal, Barbie went to Belgium in 1967 to take possession of a shipment of arms that the supplier thought would go to the Bolivian army, but Barbie sold them to, of all places, the state of Israel. As Barbie built power, he made no secret of his presence in La Paz. "Don Klaus" ate breakfast at the same café each morning, freely traveled the country in the safe company of his personal thugs, and offered his services to prospective dictator. He had no problem finding clients. Garcia Meza, the president of Bolivia in 1981 was one of them. Meza's chief of military intelligence called Barbie "my teacher."

An Uneasy Democracy: 1982–present

Meza was overthrown in a coup in 1981 and a rapid succession of military dictators followed him—three in a matter of months, plus two more within a year. Finally, in 1982, the dictator handed power back to the congress, who reinstated the results of the elections from two years earlier, bringing a legally elected civilian to power for the first time in 18 years and ushering democracy into Bolivia that has lasted to the present. Hernán Siles Zuazo instituted a "populist democracy," but the $5 billion foreign debt incurred by the military plunged the country into crisis as drought, floods, and an IMF austerity program brought acute food shortages. Inflation rose to 2,000%, then to 8,000%. With six cabinets and 75 ministers in his three years as president, Siles faced the prospect of a military coup.

Instead of another coup, the 77-year old Victor Paz Estenssoro was elected to serve a fourth term, from 1985–89, narrowly defeating Hugo Banzer. Paz reinstituted conservative economic policies, devaluing the currency, eliminating wage and price controls, and limiting government spending. Labor unions suffered once again as Paz dismantled state control of mining and gas.

The elections of 1989 saw almost equal numbers of votes cast for Hugo Banzer, Gonzalo Sánchez de Lozada ("Goni"—a conservative former economics minister), and Jaime Paz Zamora. With no candidate receiving 50% of the vote, congress elected Paz Zamora. Paz Zamora continued the policies of his uncle, Paz Estenssoro, using an IMF model of economic policy and a similar attitude toward labor unions.

Sánchez de Lozada was elected for a term in 1993–97 and again in 2002. A wealthy mine owner, he took Bolivia through some new and interesting changes called the Popular Participation Laws, which included devolving political power to local levels. Under Sánchez de Lozada, the number of locally-elected municipal officials rose ten-fold. Vigilance committees with grass-

Flamingo standing in the lake at Uyuni. Image © Javarman

roots representation have power to oversee those governments and have impeachment power over corrupt and inefficient public officials. The committees include a range of legal local organizations, from urban neighborhoods to indigenous communities. For the first time, local governments control their own budgets, subject to public oversight. An electoral slate of one-third women is required for municipal elections. Indigenous Bolivians, excluded from power for almost all of Bolivian history, have come to represent one sixth of municipal officials.

Based on his passage of politically and socially liberal laws, one might think that Sánchez de Lozada was a political hero, but many Bolivians remembered his economic shocks when he was the planning minister under Paz Estenssoro and which continued as president. Goni's solution to economic problems was a textbook case of conservative IMF economic policies. He dealt with an economy that had 8,170% inflation in the first half of 1985. A loaf of bread that cost $1.00 would cost $9.00 six months later and $83.00 in a year. A tank of gasoline that cost $20.00 one day would cost $1,654.00 a year later and $10,343.00 in two years. Production was plummeting and the government bankrupt. He reduced state spending in part by laying off 23,000 out of 30,000 miners. A third of all export earnings returned to first-world banks as repayment of debt. The unions objected to Goni because he privatized the national oil industry, water utilities, and the telephone system.

Chaos followed when Sánchez de Lozada proposed a tax increase in February of 2003. Word spread quickly in La Paz among police precincts. Soon the police joined hundreds of protesters in Plaza Murillo. The traditional conflict between the police and the army burst forth unexpectedly. When the government called out the army, a two-day shoot out with police ensued. Sánchez de Lozada was smuggled out of the presidential palace in an ambulance.

Goni Sánchez de Lozada finally relented under the blockades in 2003. There was almost no gasoline in La Paz and store shelves were increasingly bare. Coca farmers objected to him because he sent the army into the Chapare area near Cochabamba to pull up coca plants, making the U.S. eradication effort in Bolivia the most successful in the Andes at the time. Road blockades were widespread over most Bolivian cities. Goni epitomized the extreme wealth of a few and the power of foreigners to steer the course of the country.

Sánchez de Lozada turned over leadership to the vice president, Carlos Mesa, a TV journalist who Goni chose as a nonpoliticized running mate. Mesa governed for only a year and a half as unrest continued and was then replaced for six months by the chief justice of the Supreme Court until elections were held in 2005.

Those elections were won by Evo Morales. South America's first indigenous president, Morales was head of the coca growers' union. His party, the MAS (*Movimiento al Socialismo*) has moved Bolivia on a far-leftward swing. He renationalized the oil and gas industries, eased pressure against growing coca, and has taken a strong anti-U.S. position. He befriended Venezuela's Hugo Chávez, Cuba's Fidel Castro, and Ecuador's populist president Rafael Correa. Perhaps most controversially, he has attempted to change Bolivia's constitution to secure greater rights for native Bolivians, to enshrine ownership of natural resources to the government, to give indigenous systems of justice the same status as Bolivian courts, and to move federal government functions from Sucre to La Paz. This, together with cutting oil tax revenues to regional governments, has precipitated a strong conflict between the Bolivian *departamentos* (states) and the federal government.

Time will tell if Bolivia's history of extreme swings of government has begun to stabilize, though with such wide-ranging issues as indigenous power, government control of natural resources, and socialism vs. market economics, it seems unlikely.

Four

ECONOMY AND SOCIETY:
SOME PROBLEMS, SOME GAINS

Economy

Positive features of Bolivia's economy include a healthy increase in exports from natural gas and the resulting government revenues, some improvements in the mining sector, and a decrease in national debt. Unfortunately, the conflict about whether regional or federal government has the power to spend those increased gas revenues has helped to precipitate a constitutional crisis. The conflict between foreign investment and socialism continues to play out because of the important role foreign companies play in the oil and gas industry.

The country's economy has seen modest growth in the last decade—about 3%, but there are several qualifiers. Compared to recent growth of Brazil, Chile, and Peru, the growth is small. When population growth and an increase in the labor force are factored in, these economic gains diminish. Population growth is almost 2%, resulting in GDP per capita growth of only 1%. The aging of the large youthful population leads to a 3% annual increase in the labor force. Thus, Bolivia's economy needs to see strong growth to result in actual, substantial income benefits to everyday people.

The large number of people of working age relative to slow per capita economic growth results in considerable emigration. Marcela López Levy, a former researcher at the Latin American Bureau of OXFAM, writes that: "Conservative estimates put the population living abroad at 25% of all Bolivians. In other words, some two and a half million have left their country; more than one million live in Argentina, some 800,000 in the USA [many near Washington, DC] and the rest mostly in Brazil and Chile. More than half of all Bolivians have at least one family member living outside the country." At $860 million, the value of remittances from abroad far outstrip money earned from gas.

Savings, the traditional source of internal investment, have recently shown strong increases—savings as a percent of GDP rose from 4% in 1986 to 26% in 2006—but these are national savings and result from recent government nationalization of the oil and gas industry. Personal savings (the money that individuals and families actually save from income) are quite low and are the traditional source of investment capital in banks to re-loan for business creation and expansion.

National debt, long a source of concern, has decreased for two reasons. One is of course the increased government revenues from nationalization of oil and gas, and the other is debt cancellation, mostly by the Inter-American Development Bank (whose loans were equal to 10% of GDP); by the World Bank; and by the U.S. government. All three have completely cancelled their Bolivian debt.

Bolivia has experienced strong growth in exports. Exports increased 85% in the last decade due largely to zinc, Bolivia's largest metal export, as well as silver, gas, and soy. These exports have outpaced imports (consisting mostly of food, hydrocarbon processing equipment, and capital goods) resulting in a strong net positive current accounts balance and reversing negative account balances of the 1990s.

But the big issue for the Bolivian economy is the tension between foreign investment and socialism. Understanding this topic necessitates a look at Bolivia's mineral, oil, and natural gas industries.

Natural gas has replaced the combined metals and mineral industries as the country's leading revenue producer. The most valuable metals produced by Bolivia are (in order): zinc, tin, gold, silver, lead, antimony, and tungsten. The most valuable industrial minerals are (in order): boron, amethyst, and barite. Unfortunately, most of these exports are in the form of crude ores and concentrates, with low value added. While the prices of these materials have generally remained high or increased in the last several years, it is natural gas that has fueled the boom in Bolivian mineral exports. Natural gas alone accounts for 35% of total exports and a windfall in government revenues.

It is important to understand that the oil and gas industries, until recently, were all foreign-owned, and with the socialism of Evo Morales, the investment those industries brought has decreased and the prospect for further investment is dim. Producers of oil are all foreign: Petrobrás (Brazil), Repsol (Spain), BG Group (UK), British Petroleum (UK), BRIDAS (Argentina), and Pluspetrol Bolivia (Argentina). A similar story holds for ownership of Bolivian reserves of natural gas: with Repsol (Spain) controlling 34%, Total (France) 13%, BP 7% (UK), Exxon Mobil 5% (USA), and BRIDAS 4% (Argentina).

Bolivians' strong feelings about foreign control of natural resources deepened in 2006 when President Morales decreed that a majority of oil and gas production must be Bolivian owned. He even sent soldiers to oil and gas wells, not that they were needed for any military operations, but to show the strength of his intentions. Street demonstrations during 2003–2006 strongly favored nationalization. The result is that companies have withdrawn invest- ments, ceased developing new fields, and stopped all gas exploration. The repatriation of these companies' investments is so large that it results in a net divestment in gross capital formation for the country as a whole.

But there is a positive side to the increased nationalization of the oil and gas industry. Public-sector revenues have increased from 28% of GDP in 2004 to 40% in 2006, the period over which Morales strengthened government control of the oil and gas industry. Morales spent some of the money on new programs aimed at reducing poverty, such as free school lunches and money paid to mothers to keep their children in school. Some of the gas revenues have gone unspent because the current constitution gives control of them to municipal and state governments. Thus, the subject of gas earnings leads to regional political conflicts and Morales's attempts to change the constitution so that the federal government would gain a greater share of lucrative gas exports.

The mineral industry mostly follows what happens in the oil and gas industry. The large and expanding producers of minerals are foreign-owned. Bolivian-owned producers tend to be small cooperatives with no capital to invest in more efficient technology, or small private companies. These small operations are mostly involved in production of antimony and tin, and to a lesser extent, silver, lead, gold, and zinc. The two newest silver mining developments are the San Cristóbal silver mine in the far southwest which is being developed by Apex Silver Mines (Canada) and the San Bartolome project near Potosí owned by Coeur d'Alene Mines (USA). A major zinc mine is being developed by COMSUR, now renamed Sinchi Wayra (Switzerland).

Another form of the tension between foreign investment and socialism is privatization. While the economic pendulum has currently swung to nationalization, conservative economic policies between 1985 and 2003 dictated that the government shed assets that could be managed by private enterprise. Thus, Lloyd Aero Boliviano is owned by Brazilians. Telecoms were privatized too. The most dramatic conflict privatization has caused was over the proposed commercial control of water in Cochabamba in 2000. *Campesinos*, unions, activists, and those protesting what would have been much more expensive water staged street protests and met police with rocks and barricades. Foreign businesses such as MacDonald's and Firestone have sometimes been the target of anger directed at foreign control.

If Bolivia can create stable political and economic conditions to attract foreign investment, or use state revenues efficiently to provide domestic investment, the minerals industry. Instead of exporting raw ores and concentrates, Bolivia could export finished products and processed metals and chemicals. Perhaps someday your watch and camera batteries themselves will be produced in Bolivia instead of only the lithium inside them.

A huge part of Bolivia's economy is informal. About a third of the population depends on small trading transactions carried out on the street by ubiquitous indigenous people, often women. These market-savvy traders ply urban areas, bus stations, and places where traffic stops to pay road tolls, selling food, drinks, batteries, or any little item. The informal economy includes artisans producing and selling jewelry and textiles, women working as domestic laborers cooking and cleaning, ice cream vendors, phone card salesmen, young men hawking newspapers at traffic lights, and shoe-shine boys, some wearing masks so that their compatriots don't see them at such a lowly task or to protect themselves from the vapors of polish. Many of the stalls and stretches of sidewalk are controlled by a system of guilds or unions and vendors do pay for permits.

There are many advantages to the informal economy. Much of the money is earned by women who spend it on children and families. There are few barriers to become a trader and it requires little capital or education. Another significant plus of the informal economy is an end-run around heavy Bolivian bureaucracy. It can take a long time and cost a lot of money to open a business in Bolivia. To examine the effect of bureaucracy on opening a business in Peru, the Peruvian economist Hernando De Soto and his research team opened a garment workshop on the outskirts of Lima. It took them 289 days to register their business at a cost 31 times the monthly minimum wage.

Disadvantages of the informal economy include the fact that most informal traders either don't pay taxes or understate their earnings and pay few taxes, although even those with jobs in the formal economy evade taxes. This in turn lowers government revenues that could be spent on education, roads, or health care. Participants in the informal economy typically do not contribute to formal health or pension plans, so rely on savings and family support for health care and old age.

Rural altiplano *village*

With 40% of the population engaged in agriculture producing only 14% of GDP, either an even larger share of rural people must migrate to cities or abroad, or economic development solutions will need to include rural agriculture. Agricultural extension services to farmers have improved, but in the past were woefully inadequate, with only one agricultural extension agent for thousands of farmers.

Land

A serious underlying problem in Bolivia is access to land for the poor. Secure land titles are enormously important for the poor. They are the storehouse of wealth in developed countries, typically the single biggest source of wealth for a family. When owners have land title, there is incentive to improve the property, for the money spent on improvement accrues to the owners and inheritees. The land can be put up as collateral for a loan to start or improve a business. Hernando de Soto calls land not held with a secure title "dead capital," and estimates that it is five times the value of the Peruvian stock market.

The highland indigenous traditionally manage land through *ayllus*. *Ayllus* were, and still are, groups of related kin who allocate labor, land, and water to manage land and herds. The right to pasture one's animals, for example, is decided in the *ayllu* group, and boundaries are rigidly enforced. There is no traditional concept of private property ownership, nor titles or deeds. The stage was set for a conflict with western civilization. Since the coming of the Spanish, the indigenous have lost land to the western legal institution of private property, usually through the state commandeering communal lands and then selling them to whites or mestizos.

There were two significant attempts at land reform, the first by Paz Estenssoro and the MNR's efforts in the 1950s and the second by Sánchez de Lozada in 1996. The injustice of 6% of the population controlling 92% of arable land in 1952 led the MNR to arm the indigenous and encourage them to seize *haciendas*. Within a year, the Agrarian Reform Commission more formally distributed land to *campesinos' sindicatos* and *communidades*, and compensated landlords with bonds. The 1950s land reform and the expansion in the eastern lowlands were connected, for the MNR planned that landowners who lost land in the highlands would take large tracts of land in the lowlands and produce soy, corn, and cotton, providing a source of exports and modernizing Bolivian agriculture. But Peter was robbed to pay Paul, for the

large eastern landholdings were themselves taken from indigenous tribes, albeit in areas of lower population density. Much land
ended up in the hands of the military, political cronies, and other
already-capitalized individuals such as large ranchers and
sawmill operators. The stage was set for a march in 1990 that
began in Trinidad's town square. Intending to send a message
about land to La Paz, a small band of 300 (from eight ethnic
groups) walked from Trinidad to the capital, 300 miles (475 km).
It took them a month and by the time they arrived in La Paz,
there were 800 marchers. The newspapers fully covered the event
and the protestors were able to secure an agreement with President Jaime Paz Zamora, who signed a decree that created the
Multiethnic Indigenous Territory. The document recognized
indigenous land as collective property. However, a few years after
the march, a gap was evident between rights on paper and secure
land tenure for *campesinos*.

Large landholdings remained and so a second effort at land
reform came in 1996 under Sánchez de Lozada. This 1996 agrarian reform recognized collective land ownership with legal land
titles, both in the highlands and lowlands. Small-holders were
not required to pay taxes, but medium- and large-sized were.
With bureaucratic corruption and power of the wealthy, the
depth of the reform is still a work in progress.

Poverty, Education, and Health

Income is not well distributed across social classes. It reflects the
ethnicity of a large native population and a history of economic
domination by white Bolivians and foreigners. The poorest 10% of
Bolivians earn 0.3% of GDP; the richest 10% earn 47%. (The
corresponding figures for the U.S. are 2% and 30%, respectively.)
This gap is the source of much social tension.

A joint effort among UDAPE (the Unidad de Análisis de
Politicas Sociales y Económicas), the World Bank, and the Boli-
vian National Statistics Institute (Instituto Naciona Estadística de
Bolivia) mapped and analyzed regional differences in poverty.

Rural farmer in the Andes. Image © Photochris

Areas of the highest poverty have between 83% to almost 100% of the population living below the poverty line. Even areas of low poverty range from 22% to 43%. Poverty is a profound national problem in Bolivia.

The geography of Bolivian poverty was mapped by Colombia University's CIESEN (the Center for International Earth Science Information Network). It shows that the areas of least poverty are cities and towns, together with the eastern lowlands and Tarija to the south. The greatest poverty is in rural areas and highland mining districts.

One result is widespread internal migration. López Levy cites evidence that at least a million people have migrated to other parts of the country in the 1990s alone. Between emigration and internal migration, half the population has migrated. Migration patterns show a strong rural-to-urban trend and a west-to-east movement. Probably no city has experienced such strong in-migration as El Alto, the indigenous city above La Paz. When El Alto became a city in 1985, it had a population of 95,000. A mere 20 years later it had a population of 825,000. One can imagine the strain such growth puts on schools, hospitals, and social services.

Education underwent significant changes beginning in 1994 as a result of the Popular Participation laws under President Goni Sánchez de Lozada. The Popular Participation laws in general devolved political power to municipalities, increased their funding from 10% to 20% of federal government revenues, and created local governance bodies for schools and local organizations. It gave local councils the power to allocate resources, and increased the role of women and the indigenous in governance.

Education before 1994 was fraught with problems. Manuel Contreras, a specialist in social development at the Inter-American Bank, and Maria Luisa Talavera, a Bolivian ethnographic education researcher, describe it: "Through three decades, there was no single entity with either viable proposals or the political strength to carry out needed reforms. There was a lack of capacity to tackle the key structural issues of a very weak MEC [the Education Ministry], an outdated curriculum, very low levels of teacher competence and training, or to confront the strength of the teachers' unions."

Educational gains after 1994 happened in several ways. Indigenous children are now often taught in their native languages—previously, all instruction was only in Spanish, contributing to very high dropout rates. Pedagogy became less lecture-based with less emphasis on rote learning. A new curriculum and teacher guides were offered. Citizens participated in decisions about the schools. Educational spending rose as well, rising from 2.7% of GDP in the early 1990s to 5.0% in 2000 and

6.4% in 2007. Teachers' salaries increased too, at a rate about double that of inflation.

Teachers' unions are very strong in Bolivia and have been a major impediment to improving education. Education unions had quite different goals than the Ministry of Education. The unions wanted to strengthen class consciousness, maintain different urban and rural school standards, guarantee teacher employment, increase salaries without links to productivity, make union membership mandatory to all teachers, and limit school board and parental participation. The urban union resisted the changes of 1994 more than the rural union, who worked more closely with ministry technicians. Popular Participation has brought the unions more in line with needs of parents and local school boards.

Like education, what's new in Bolivian health care is largely tied to the mid-1990's Popular Participation. Since then, Bolivian health has focused on maternal and infant health, both urban and rural. The presence of trained personnel at births has more than doubled, from 24% in 1994 to 54% in 2002. The World Bank study of Bolivian health in 2004 noted two concerns surrounding this: that recently, the increase has tapered off and that the equity gap remains—"the coverage of skilled birth attendance was 89% for the richest fifth of the population, while it reached only 25% for the poorest." In addition, the rural/urban differences in delivery of maternal and infant health remain large.

Public health is actually a combination of public, private, and non-profit sectors, and the social security system. About half of the population uses the Basic Health Insurance program, which has two focuses. One is maternal and infant care, and the other is directed at communicable and vector-borne diseases, Bolivia's largest killer. Called the Epidemiological Shield, the program concentrates on child immunizations and highly prevalent diseases such as Chagas and malaria (caused by parasites) and tuberculosis (a bacteria), which together comprise 40% of disease in Bolivia. Those three diseases affect the poor more than the rich and are estimated to lower GDP by 7%.

One limiting factor on Bolivian health is a shortage of doctors and nurses. At 6.6 doctors and 3.4 nurses per 10,000 people, Bolivia's health staff is about half the Latin American average. Again, there is a geographical imbalance, with many urban areas having sufficient staff of doctors (but still a shortage of nurses), but too few of both in rural areas.

Politics

The constitutional changes proposed by Evo Morales and the MAS (*Movimiento al Socialismo*) encapsulate politics in the first decade of the 21st century. The details of the proposed revision span the core issues in Bolivian politics today.

Morales's changes would enshrine state ownership of natural resources into the constitution. Hydrocarbons are the first ground tested by nationalization, and mining could follow. The indigenous would be empowered by putting traditional native systems of justice on a par with the existing judiciary. The constitutional tribunal would have equal numbers of indigenous and non-indigenous and become a fourth branch of government. Bolivia would be self-described as a plurinational state, but in practice this would make little difference since the Bolivian constitution already identifies the country as multi-ethnic.

Another proposed change would give greater autonomy to departments and municipalities, a point demanded by the political opposition, although it would also decrease their share of revenues from natural resources. It is difficult to predict how this power struggle between the west and east will resolve itself. The Santa Cruz department, which leads the opposition to Morales, has proposed statutes that would create its own legislature, construct its own police force, raise its own taxes for public works, and negotiate its own royalty agreements for oil and gas. One provision of Morales's constitutional changes includes a referendum on whether or not any landholder could own up to 25,000 acres (10,000 hectares). The 1953 agrarian laws of Victor Paz Estenssoro limited land holdings in the highlands but were never applied to the lowlands.

Sucre, The White City

The most contentious of the MAS's constitutional changes embed power of their party and Evo Morales. They would change the composition of the congress by lowering the number of deputies and raising the number of senators, thereby decreasing the power of the opposition. The president would be re-elected after ratification of the constitutional changes, but Morale's first term as president would neither count toward the two-term limit, nor would it violate the present prohibition on consecutive terms. In order to get their proposed changes ratified, the MAS proposes that ratification be validated by two thirds of members present, not two thirds of members elected. The ratification process has been ugly. MAS party members first met in Sucre, maintaining that they represented a two thirds majority—party thugs frightened away the opposition. When that provoked street riots, they moved the meeting to a military academy outside Sucre and surrounded it with troops and MAS supporters. Unable to return safely to Sucre, the MAS moved the meeting to Oruro where their support was stronger. Political opposition parties were once again not present in Oruro, where they "approved" the new constitution. The political opposition did not recognize that as ratification.

Another issue surrounding proposed constitutional changes concerns Sucre. Sucre was once Bolivia's capital but later became the seat of the judiciary only, with the executive and legislative bodies operating in La Paz. The proposed constitutional changes do not say where these bodies would be located, but Sucre wants to be sure it doesn't lose the function it has now. The conflict is more than geographical—the underlying problem is whether the authority to change the constitution rests with the president or the congress.

U.S. and Bolivia

The history of U.S.–Bolivian relations has not been a happy one. Many Bolivians are suspicious of the U.S. for reasons spanning interference in internal political and economic policies, to the U.S. relation with the Bolivian army and the role the U.S. has played in coca eradication.

The first U.S. diplomatic contact by John Appleton, a chargé d'affaires sent by Secretary of State James Buchanan in 1848, is described by Kenneth Lehman, a specialist on relations between the U.S. and Bolivia:

> If North American confidence was high in 1848, it did not remain at that level. Appleton quickly discovered the limits of his ability to influence this distant neighbor of the United States. His first problems were basic and personal. He reported back to Washington soon after arriving in Bolivia that the country had only two North American residents, no cart roads, and a climate so "unfriendly" to his health that he wished to be recalled at the earli-

est convenience. More crucial to his diplomatic mission, he could find no government to whom he could present his credentials.

The authority to which Appleton eventually did find to receive his credentials was Manuel Isidoro Belzú. Belzú and many other Bolivians distrusted the U.S. as a territorial imperialist as they watched the U.S. Navy explore the Rio de la Plata through Paraguay to Bolivia's borders in 1852; as two U.S. naval officers explored the tributaries of the Amazon in direct opposition to Brazil in the same year; as the U.S. forced the opening of Japan in 1854; and as American William Walker tried to take over Central America in 1857. When one of the U.S. naval officers who was exploring the Amazon visited La Paz, a well-educated woman asked him if he wanted Bolivia too. Belzú also distrusted the British as economic imperialists and imposed tariffs on British goods, pointing out that Britain had done the same in its mercantilist period.

Little happened between the U.S. and Bolivia over the next 30 years—only 50 North Americans were present in Bolivia by the mid-1870s and trade was miniscule. However, when the U.S. Civil War ended in 1865, Americans made minor investments in Mariano Melgarejo's Bolivia: in stagecoaches, railroads, a bank, and a mint at Potosí, but all vestiges of those investments were gone by 1880.

Nothing had improved by 1890. The few U.S. investments in Bolivia included George Church's failed railroad to exploit Amazon rubber. Three railroads from Bolivia to the Pacific did exist by the turn of the century, built by U.S. companies and then leased to British ones, but as ore went out, imports came in, so that Peruvian sugar and California wheat cost half that from Santa Cruz or Cochabamba. Britain refined Bolivian tin, reaping the greater value added from processing. Bolivians remained distrustful of U.S. foreign intentions. Kenneth Lehman:

In 1895, Richard Olney [U.S. Attorney General] made his famous assertion of U.S. hegemony in the Venezuelan border affair: "Today the United States is practically sovereign on this continent [hemisphere] and its fiat is law upon the subjects of

which it confines its interposition." Both the successes of the
United States and its proximity to Latin America made it so.
In the years that followed Olney's declaration, the United
States intervened in Cuba, took a colony in Puerto Rico,
fomented a revolution in Panama, began to work on an isth-
mian canal, and unilaterally declared its right to intervene in
the affairs of its neighbors for their own good.

It was finally WWI that would increase trade between the
U.S. and Bolivia, almost all of it tin and oil. Bolivian exports to the
U.S. grew from a mere $200,000 in 1913 to $35 million in 1918. By
the 1920s, Standard Oil began investing in Bolivia and controlled
oil production within the decade. At first, to raise investment capital to drill for oil, U.S. banks loaned Bolivia $33 million. Lehman:
"In exchange for a $33 million loan, Bolivia pledged its customs
receipts as security and, to guarantee payment, agreed to create a
three-member Permanent Fiscal Commission (two if its members
to be chosen by the U.S. banks) to collect taxes over the twenty-
five-year life of the loan." By 1927 after more loans, "U.S. banks
collected Bolivia's taxes, oversaw customs receipts, and played a
direct role in setting government fiscal policies."

Tin contracts exemplify the uneven relations between the U.S.
and Bolivia. Tin was the single biggest basis of U.S.–Bolivian relations from WWI to the end of the Korean War in 1953. The price
of tin had fluctuated widely over a long period of time so it was in
Bolivia's interest to forge contracts that would at least guarantee a
price higher than production costs, but the U.S. agreed to such
contracts only in times of war when it was in the U.S.'s best interest. During WWII when demand for tin was high and the U.S.
and British governments bid on prices for tin, the U.S. raised the
price it paid from 48¢ per pound to 63¢ but other countries such as
Argentina paid much more, leading some Bolivian historians to
calculate that the price would have risen faster on an open market.
A Bolivian minister, Mariano Baptista Gumucio, "calculated
Bolivia's losses at $670,315,000—far more than the total of all U.S.
aid to Bolivia through the 1960s." After WWII the U.S. used its tin

stockpiles and government-buying contracts to keep the price of tin low, leading Bolivian trade negotiator and ambassador Víctor Andrade to bitterly complain that Bolivia's alliance with the U.S. was at a huge cost to Bolivia. Tungsten was a similar story.

The U.S. gave Bolivia considerable foreign aid after WWII during the Paz Estenssoro turnaround, that built highways, including the first paved road from the highlands to Santa Cruz, and invested in public health in malarial areas. This effort was designed by the U.S. to weaken communist power and was coupled with overt efforts to engineer breaks between the MNR and the more radical parties—efforts that were successful.

In the late 1960s, U.S. aid policy changed from giving Bolivia food aid to giving it loans. U.S. loans in 1969 required that Bolivia "spend an amount equivalent to all loans received on U.S.-made products. The requirement, designed to ease mounting U.S. balance-of-payments problems, forced Bolivia to pay up to three times more for American goods than for comparable goods produced in Japan or Europe."

In economic matters, the U.S. has pushed conservative policies for decades. The U.S. withheld aid in 1959, 1972, and 1986 when it looked as though Bolivia would renege on the IMF-sponsored path. Most of the U.S. aid in the 1960s was surplus U.S. food that depressed prices that Bolivian farmers could get. Altogether, many Bolivians saw U.S. efforts as serving primarily U.S. interests and as attempts to meddle in their internal affairs.

Besides U.S. influence on internal Bolivian politics and economic policies, the U.S. role in the Bolivian army and the drug trade have dominated the relationship. Beginning in the Paz Estenssoro years, part of the aid package included implementing U.S. plans to reorganize the army. U.S. President Kennedy increased military aid 800%, but stipulated that the Bolivian military build roads, airstrips, and schools, and conduct literacy and medical campaigns. Training was also given at the School of the Americas. By 1963, 659 Bolivian military officers were trained—more military training was provided to Bolivians at Ft. Benning, Georgia, than to any other country.

When the cocaine trade got to be a major issue in the 1980s, the U.S. financed an arm of the Bolivian military to destroy coca plants, the plant that produces cocaine. Not all U.S.–Bolivian relations in the army were bad. In 1988, Bolivia passed Law 1008, concerning cocaine. Law 1008 was passed with the influence of the Reagan presidency during the Bolivian presidencies of Paz Estenssoro and Hernán Siles Zuazo in the 1980s. It has been highly contentious in Bolivia. Law 1008 provides for a separate legal system to prosecute cocaine producers and traffickers; curbs coca-producing areas; and sets provisions for U.S. aid based on coca eradication. The law creates an anti-drug unit of the Bolivian military that works closely with the U.S. Drug Enforcement Agency. Many of the details of coca eradication have been kept secret from the Bolivian public. Eduardo Gamarra, Director of the Latin American and Caribbean Center in Florida, writes: "Counternarcotics activities were planned by the United States with little or no Bolivian input. The Bolivian government agreed to implement policies in secret to avoid political costs. All 'secret' initiatives inevitably became public, revealing that most were unconstitutional." Over $14 million of U.S. aid was contingent on passing Law 1008.

Law 1008 was pushed through the Bolivian congress quickly, with little time for review. Congress did attach a provision that prohibited the use of chemicals to kill coca plants, so the U.S.-financed arm of the Bolivian military pulled up coca plants, to the chagrin of farmers who make more money from coca than alternative crops. Coca is not consumed as cocaine in Bolivia, but as harmless coca leaf, so many Bolivians see the U.S. eradication effort as yet another policy that serves U.S. rather than Bolivian needs.

Relations between the U.S. and Bolivia remain problematic. Tools in the U.S. diplomatic arsenal include suspending rules that allow duty-free and low-tariff preferences on Bolivian goods, and curtailing $85 million in annual aid. Bolivian diplomatic weapons include expulsion of DEA agents and the U.S. ambassador (which the Bolivians did in 2008 because the ambassador met with lowland opposition governors).

Tea pickers working in the Yungas region. Image © Jrothe

Five

CULTURE AND RELIGION:
UNIQUE BOLIVIA

Coca

Few subjects are as important to understanding Bolivia as coca. The coca plant is a shrub-sized bush with citrus-like leaves that contains trace amounts of cocaine. The most important thing to say about coca is what the Bolivians say: *coca no es cocaine*. Coca leaf is not addictive and is widely used in Bolivia. Cocaine, however, is highly addictive and is a serious social and health problem in the developed world (and in those countries that transport cocaine). Cocaine was refined from coca leaf in 1860 by Europeans. From the Bolivians' point of view, the cocaine problem was created by outsiders who now pay the Bolivian military to uproot coca plants, the source of income for many thousands of poor Bolivians. Most Bolivians see the U.S. war on cocaine as being a foreign problem for which Bolivians pay the price.

Coca has been grown in the Andes for 4,500 years. All pre-Hispanic people of the Andes have left evidence of coca use. Three thousand year old ceramic figures have the puffed-out cheeks of the coca chewer. Legends from the highlands in Colombia describe how people descended from the Milky Way in a canoe, carrying coca. The Inca believed that a fellow named The Original Inca gave birth to their civilization in union with Pachamama, and their daughter was Mama Coca. Coca leaves were found buried with a mummified corpse on the *altiplano* dating from 2500 B.C. Coca leaf was used in ceremonies and by the nobility before the Spanish, then became more widely used when the Spanish put natives to work in the mines and *haciendas*.

Coca has historically been used at high altitudes. Seventy-five percent of the high-elevation population presently chews coca, compared to 20% at moderate elevations and 3% at low altitude, though its use is spreading in the lowlands as *altiplano* Quechua and Aymara move to the eastern lowlands seeking land and jobs. Coca, however, cannot be grown on the *altiplano*, but only at moderate and lower elevations in the transition zone between highland and lowland, so the Yungas is the traditional area of production. Most Yungas leaf is chewed, but when the east-west highway opened in the 1970s, it opened the Chapare region to coca production and much of that is made into cocaine.

Coca is ideally suited to the Yungas. It grows on nutrient-poor soils and can be harvested through the year. Once the labor-intensive mounding of soil is done, the resultant ridges along contour lines retard soil erosion. *Campesinos* do often use fertilizer and pesticides, however, in excessive amounts and without precautions, even mixing the chemicals with their hands. Repeated fertilizer use leaves salts behind, degrading the soil. Pesticides may affect many animals, especially birds.

Coca leaf is consumed in the following ways. The user grasps a coca leaf by the stem and pulls the stem between top and bottom teeth, stripping the leaf off to remain in the mouth, then discarding the sharp stem. This process is repeated until a small wad of coca leaf accumulates in the cheek. The user then bites off a small amount of *lejia*. *Lejia* is made from burnt vegetables, usually grain or banana, and is necessary to chemically release the trace amounts of cocaine alkaloid in the leaf. Coca leaf is also consumed as tea, as coca candy available at the Coca Museum in the Witches' Market in La Paz, or in soft drinks in Peru.

The effects of chewing coca leaf are primarily a reduction in appetite and a willingness to start work and to work longer. It is also used as to relieve the effects of high elevation, since it imperceptibly stimulates both the frequency and depth of breathing, thereby increasing the amount of oxygen in the blood. Coca leaf is used in the Andes as a stomach remedy and a poultice for skin injuries.

Coca leaf is not addictive. Dr. Jorge Hurtado Gumucio, who founded the Coca Museum in La Paz, runs Bolivia's largest psychiatric hospital and is an expert on coca and cocaine. He has never witnessed withdrawal symptoms from patients who enter the hospital and who stop chewing coca leaf. He points out that someone who chews coca leaf all day long consumes one twentieth the amount of cocaine that an addict get in one dose, and that the addict gets a blast which then translates to a depressive effect as the cocaine wears off. Such a coming-down is not observed in the leaf chewer. The addict can take in large amounts of cocaine while the dose of the leaf chewer is inherently limited and cannot be exceeded. Dr. Hurtado has even prescribed coca leaf as part of a therapy for cocaine addicts, even though it is very clear that cocaine is powerfully addictive and is a social scourge.

Coca production peaked in the late 1980s and early 1990s when prices of cocaine were at their highest. At that time, economists estimated that coca and cocaine were one-quarter of Bolivian GNP. Now, Bolivian coca production is greatly reduced, from almost 50,000 hectares in the early 1990s to less than 20,000 in the early 2000s, largely due to eradication in the Chapare and Yapacaní northeast of Cochabamba. The U.S. coca eradication program applies to all Andean countries, but has been most successful in Bolivia with the cooperation of présidents Hugo Banzer and Goni Sánchez de Lozada. Coca eradication programs are completely due to the U.S. European countries contribute to the effort to find alternative crops, but only the U.S. finances coca crop destruction, so it is the U.S. who bears the brunt of Bolivian frustration.

Alternative crops are obviously critical in the effort to reduce the amount of land planted to coca, although the success of alternative crops is widely agreed to be a failure, because while the crops can be produced, there isn't a market for them. The U.S. has tried oranges, coffee, palm hearts, pineapples, soybeans, chilies, passion fruit, papaya, bananas, plantains, tomatoes, and racacha (a potato-like vegetable). Unfortunately, none can equal the return from coca, nor sometimes even generate enough to feed a family.

Coca farms in the Yungas. Image © by Totorean

Roads are poor and products far from markets. The U.S. abandoned plans to foster soybeans and citrus in Bolivia when the
powerful U.S. farm interests lobbied against them in Congress.

The U.S. has consistently threatened to withhold aid if the Bolivian government does not meet coca eradication targets. The U.S.
ambassador to Bolivia in 2000-02, Manuel Rocha, infuriated Bolivians when he suggested that if the pro-coca political candidate Evo

Morales was elected in the presidential elections, that the U.S. would cease aid altogether. Morales in turn said that Rocha was his best supporter—the more Rocha angered Bolivians, the more they voted for Morales. Morales came in a very close second in the 2002 election and won it in 2005. His position is to allow traditional use of coca leaf while eliminating cocaine production and trafficking.

The U.S. government spends $185 million a year in Bolivia. Ninety-one million goes to the coca-eradication program. Eighty-five million goes to food aid, child health, development, economic support, the Peace Corps, and military financing. Including a hundred and fifty Peace Corps staff, the U.S. employs over a thousand people, half of whom are Bolivian. The U.S. has forgiven all Bolivian bilateral debt. Still, if one strips away the $91 million dollars for coca eradication, the amount of U.S. aid to Bolivia ranks about sixth, behind Germany, Holland, the E.U., Japan, even China. Cocaine will continue to be an important part of the future of U.S.–Bolivian relations. Unfortunately, there are no easy solutions.

Religion

Key themes to understanding religion in Bolivia are: the role of the Catholic church, the recent rise of evangelical churches, and the prevalence of native beliefs as part of widespread syncretism among the indigenous.

The history of the Catholic church in Bolivia is that of two churches. One is of the traditional Latin American conservative church, although less powerful than the colonial churches in Mexico, Peru, or Argentina, because José Antonio Sucre took much of the church's power immediately after independence in 1825. The other is the church that developed in the liberation theology of the 1960s which supports indigenous rights, speaks out against dictators, and champions the poor. Jeffrey Klaiber, a Jesuit priest and university president who lived thirty-five years in Peru, writes that before the 1960s, the church was typical of those in the Andes, "small, conservative, fearful of communism and Protestantism, and little concerned about social and political questions," but that by the 1980s, the church in Bolivia had evolved from a "typically conservative and traditional church into one of the most progressive in Latin America."

The degree to which the colonial and post-colonial church had power was revealed by the actions Sucre took against it. He confiscated church lands, the rents those lands earned, and mortgages people paid to the church. He cut church income by taking state control over tithes. Though Sucre used the wealth taken from the church to finance urban schools, the income was not large and the effect of taking them as state income did not last. Sucre decreased the size of monasteries and convents and took state ownership of their private estates. He eliminated the *cofriadías*, the elite, honorary brotherhoods who supported the church financially and helped maintain religious celebrations. Bolívar had provided for the state to approve bishops and other ecclesiastic officials and to approve or disapprove all church decrees.

Even though Sucre permanently reduced the power of the Catholic church, church and state were not separate. The first Bolivian constitution of 1826 recognized Catholicism as the religion of the state, to the exclusion of all other religions and sects. The constitution gave the government powers to approve clergy officials and required the president to be Catholic. The state contributed a small sum for clergy's salaries but did recognize land ownership by the church. Few changes were made with respect to church and state through the many constitutions, and little dissatisfaction was expressed until in 1871, when a constitutional article was changed to allow other sects. The reason was to encourage immigration.

Priests translated Quechua and Aymara into dictionaries and published grammars allowing a written language for the first time. (They translated Quechua almost a generation before Aymara, inadvertently contributing to the dominance of the Quechua language spread by missionaries.) In the eastern lowlands, Jesuits taught natives to read, to improve their agriculture, and established what is still the leading university, until they were kicked

The Catholic Churh at Copacabana

out literally overnight by the king of Spain in 1767, who feared their growing power and liberal ideas. Jesuits resettled tribes and reorganized them into towns surrounding the churches where they instituted the Spanish system of town councils. They taught natives to build musical instruments and play music—their indigenous baroque music, written by natives hundreds of years ago, is currently undergoing a revival.

One icon from colonial times stands out as the national religious symbol— the Virgin of Copacabana at the town of the same name on the shore of Lake Titicaca. The wooden statue of a few feet high was carved by the indigenous Francisco Tito Yupanqui, who began the work in Potosí 1580. He had difficulty getting priests to accept it as a legitimate religious symbol, but it was eventually installed in the church in Copacabana in 1853. Many Bolivians see her as a dark Virgin whose features validate the indigenous efforts against white oppressors. People come from all over the country to ask favors of her and walk all the way from La Paz to worship her. Similar symbols, like the Virgin of Socovón in Oruro and countless icons in small churches everywhere, play powerful roles in local religious life, especially at festivals.

A new Catholic church evolved from liberation theology and its preferential option for the poor in the 1960s. The church began to speak out on social and political issues. It became sympathetic with miners and university students. Jesuits and Oblates opened radio stations; founded *La Presencia*, an important daily national newspaper; and the church served as a forum for national dialogue. The church was called on several times to mediate between political parties or disputes between the government and striking miners. The church played this liberal and humanistic role particularly during Garcia Meza's dictatorship, using churches as sites for hunger strikes and publicizing human rights abuses of the government.

Church clergy paid heavily for opposing the dictatorships of Garcia Meza and Hugo Banzer. In 1973, 99 priests and nuns signed a document accusing Banzer's government of suppressing democracy, murder, human rights violations, and for using the courts to persecute people for their political ideas. Banzer exiled more than a hundred clergy. That same year, a priest and head of the Justice and Peace Commission offered himself to Banzer's government in exchange for five women illegally arrested for political reasons. The women were released. The church sponsored prayer vigils, jail visits, fasts, and letter-writing campaigns. In 1977-78, a hunger strike begun by four women on the premises of the La Paz archdiocese became a national crusade. Twenty-eight groups and 1,200 people joined the hunger strike as it spread to Oruro, Tarija, Sucre, and Santa Cruz. Strikers positioned them-

The Jesuit Church at San Ignacio de Moxos in Beni department

selves in churches and the offices of unions and Catholic newspapers. Perhaps the most famous liberal clergyman was Luiz Espinal, a Spanish-born Jesuit priest who founded a newspaper that denounced government corruption and identified ties between the government and drug traffickers. Espinal was kidnapped, tortured, and killed outside La Paz in 1980. His remains are buried in a prominent place near the entrance to the general cemetery in La Paz, his grave marked with a smooth, graceful gray stone carving.

The church was not unified in this liberation theology. As Klaiber writes, some clergy denounced the progressive church as representing "foreign influences and Marxist infiltration of the church." And indeed, the foreign origin of most of Bolivia's priests has only recently begun to change. Most of Bolivia's priests came from Italy, Spain, Germany, and North America. Klaiber calculates that by the late 1980s, of the 727 priests in Bolivia, 30% were Bolivian by birth and half of the 1,523 religious women were.

A notable feature of religion in Bolivia today is the rapid growth of evangelical churches. A perusal of the phone book of any Bolivian city will reveal a bewildering range of church names. Many reveal a foreign origin: from the United States, international religious organizations, or from Brazil or Europe. Some are urban churches whose well-built quality shows foreign financing. Others are poor, ramshackle buildings in tattered parts of cities or in very small towns. Some of the foreign churches operate both a church and school. With their foreign funding and disciplined staff, these schools are sometimes well-regarded by locals and offer the alternative to a low-quality and underfunded government school.

Lastly, a significant feature of religion in Bolivia concerns the indigenous population's strong syncretism and the survival of indigenous beliefs and customs. Catholic rituals are often used for baptisms, marriages, and funerals. Older traditions live on for veneration of ancestors, native spirits, and mother earth, *Pachamama*. This syncretism evolved from pre-colonial times, when the few hundred priests, sent to minister to the needs of millions, were content to accommodate many indigenous beliefs— not those associated with native creation stories, but those related to planting, harvesting, and kinship. Local village priests factored such native beliefs into rural church services, and priests would appear at indigenous rituals to celebrate, although the upper-echelons of Catholic administration discouraged such activities.

The cosmology of Andean natives shows strong ties from the past to the present, and from nature to man. For example, llama fetuses and other burnt offerings are given whenever *Pachamama* is broken into, such as planting or road building. Indigenous ceremonies acknowledge and venerate native spirits. Reverence for ancestors shows in *huacas*—little stone statues, golden figurines, silver amulets, rocks, hills, mountains, or anything the natives revered as a record of their ancestors. For after death, the spirit of an important person could readily inhabit one of these objects. *Huacas* say important things about Andean natives. One is that the world is continuous between the living and the dead. The world is alive with ancestral spirits. One sees them every day in hills and mountains above and they are present in the bones, statues, or carvings stored nearby in a shrine. Michael Moseley, archeology professor at the University of Florida, writes: "…ancestor veneration was a fundamental institution of Andean society. Native concepts did not maintain a sharp division between the living and the dead, and the deceased actively influenced the health and well-being of their descendants." Many of these beliefs and customs are readily visible in Bolivian celebrations and carnivals.

Carnival

Carnivals are the most spectacular expression of Bolivian culture. They are frequent, with most landing on Catholic church holidays. The granddaddy of them all is held in Oruro late in February, starting the week before the Catholic Ash Wednesday, though all cities have elaborate carnivals. Carnivals involve a colorful grand parade, typically led by local and church officials, some of whom carry an important religious icon on their shoulders. Blaring horns and pounding drums follow as band after band pass by, interwoven with troupes of dancers—Oruro has 48 groups of bands and dancers, parading from mid-morning until late at night. The dances of the carnivals occur only at carnivals, and the masks are not worn at any other times. Some musical instruments are buried in the earth for a year until the following year's festivities. At La Paz's biggest carnival, the God of Great Power (Señor del Gran Poder), a likeness of Punch (Pepino or Punchinello) is unearthed from the general cemetery and reburied after carnival. Vivid, symbolic costumes with elaborate masks hint at the wealth of indigenous culture.

Carnival dress representing the black slaves of the Morenada

There are hundreds of carnival dances. A few well-known ones that a visitor will often see include the morenada, which represents the black slaves brought by the Spaniards to perform domestic work, to labor in the furnaces and royal mint at Potosí, and to stomp grapes. The slaves suffered enormously from altitude sickness, reflected in the shiny, black masks whose eyes bulge and tongues hang out. Beautiful young women in short, fluffed skirts and high

Devil (Diablada) mask

heels twirl by, as do their *Cholita* mothers in orange, purple, green, violet, or magenta, followed by the main body of male Morenada dancers, then a band with brass and drums.

Another principal dance of carnival, one that originated in Oruro, is the Diablada. A high-stepping St. Michael leads a crowd of Lucifers. The Spanish priest Montealegre designed the dance as a parable that would both teach Catholicism and help cover old

Carnival mask from the east

ways. In some versions of the dance, St. Michael, dressed in white, calls up the seven deadly sins individually. The sins answer him with "Here I am" and he banishes them from the mines. Also present in the Diablada are the long-legged female devils, the condor, and the bear.

A third main dance is the Incas, a theater piece about the death of Atahualpa at the hands of Francisco Pizarro. There are also

St. Michael banishes the devils

many other dances: the Caporales, that symbolizes foremen whipping natives, whose dancers twirl noisemakers that mimic the sounds of the slaves' chains; the Tinku that ritualizes the territorial battles of areas near Potosí; the Llamadas who twirl their slings that are used to herd llamas; and there are dances from the lowlands too, easily identified by costumes from hot climates and decorated with feathers of jungle birds. The long white beards, absurdly large hats, and silly pointed shoes are a satire of the Spaniards, while the bent-over posture and crooked canes of the male dancers, and their playful behavior of complaining, simply represent the aches and pains of growing old.

The masks are huge, brightly-painted extravagances with glaring teeth and horns. Masks are made from wood, plaster, tin, copper, or fabric, with bits of mirrors and thermos flasks, sequins, trinkets, and sparkling paint, or bulging eyes made from burned-out light bulbs. White beards and smoking pipes mock the conquistadors. Shiny dragons with glaring teeth and horns extend far over the dancer's head.

One way to appreciate the importance of carnival is to consider the cost to individuals who participate. In a country whose average annual income is $4,000, it costs $250 for a Diablada costume, or six percent of income, plus after lodging, food, and travel expenses, participation in carnival is 10% of a person's income. Carnival is profoundly important to Bolivians.

Carnival also involves considerable drinking. Alcohol consumption is a deep problem in Bolivia. Drinking often lasts for the duration of carnival. Mornings reveal inebriated souls sprawled in the street.

Indigenous Culture

Because the indigenous comprise a large proportion of Bolivia's people—50% speaking a native language at home and some greater percentage under broader definitions—their customs are a significant feature of the country's cultural landscape. Visitors relish their textiles, music, local festivals, and archeology.

Textiles express native culture in vivid colors and their symbols give clues to cultural values. Textiles for indigenous people in Bolivia are not just for everyday wear, but play roles as gifts, in ceremonies, and to identify the ethnic and geographic region of the wearer. Materials range from llama, vicuña, or sheep's wool to cotton, which is native to South America. The historical role of textiles shows their importance. The Inca required cloth tributes as a form of currency to pay taxes to the emperor. The finest weavings were burned in religious and sacrificial rituals or buried with the dead, while more mundane cloth was used to clothe troops and civil servants. Incan soldiers would abandon llamas and captives on the battlefield when

Tarabuco fabrics. Image © Morton Elm

the tide turned against them, but take time to burn extensive stockpiles of textiles.

The brilliant colors of Bolivian textiles are a product of skilled dyers whose products neither fade nor bleed. Weaving is typically done by women, mostly in the winter. There are strong regional styles with respect to colors, styles, patterns, and zoomorphic motif. For example, Tarabuco fabrics use vivid reds, black, and often depict a horse. Nearby Potolo textiles depict a great variety of winged creatures, some with four legs, others headless or multi-headed. Some of their woven birds wear human clothes, and the sun god Inti is popular. The Llallagua area produces fabrics with motifs of flowers, trucks, cars, trains, and a wide range of animals.

Another vital thread of indigenous culture is music. Writing in 1912 during his extensive and brave explorations in the Andes and the Amazon, Charles Johnson Post wrote of Bolivian music:

> In the remains of the vast Indian nation shattered by Pizarro, the Empire of the Incas, every man and boy, almost from the age when he can walk, is adept on their simple reed flutes and Panandean pipes…They are a musical race; there are songs and airs for each season, for the planting, for the harvest, for the valorous deeds of the vanished caciques [Indian leaders]; for their gods of old to whom a new significance has been given by a pious Church, and the long-drawn chants by means of which, at their yearly gatherings, they pass down the history of their race. As there is no written language, there is no written music; it is handed down from generation to generation by the ear alone.

The traditional songs, especially in rural areas, are more a part of the fabric of society than in the developed world, so they are played not just for entertainment or dancing, but at baptisms, for courting, at weddings, and funerals. The tones of the songs can be happy, especially those of the eastern lowlands. There is a pervasive sadness to some on the *altiplano*, whose lyrics echo five hundred years of suffering at the hands of the Spanish, though the melancholy can also be pining for a girl who's gone to the city or an emigrant dreaming of his village.

The instruments reach out from a distant past. Clay or bone flutes, and a statue playing one, date from 900 B.C. The Spanish priest and chronicler Bernabé Cobo describes how the Incan creator Viracocha fashioned people and animals from the mud at Tiwanaku and gave them many languages so that they could sing many kinds of song. Flutes evolved from clay and bone to cane. You can sometimes hear the cry of the condor in quena flute notes. *Charangos*, modeled after the Spanish guitar, were originally made from armadillo shells, and you can still buy one with hairs sticking out of it.

The spirit of the Andes

Like paintings and carvings, like dances and carnivals, indigenous music is in a constant state of flux. Violins, guitars, and harps have long been integrated into native traditions, and now saxophones, accordions, and electric synthesizers keep new blood flowing in Andean musical veins. Lyrics can be different for the same tune and several titles can describe the same song. How close the land lies to one's heart is a theme never lost. Traditionally, voice was not part of highland music, although it is assuming an increasing role. Women rarely play any instrument, except sometimes a small drum, but their voices now sometimes contribute to the songs. Many of the best groups use their music to emigrate to Germany, the Netherlands, the U.S., and Canada.

A rather unknown attraction of indigenous Bolivia is ancient rock painting. More than a thousand rock paintings have been registered though in all *departamentos*. They range back to Wankarani culture but rock painting continued through colonial and republican times.

Paintings are of llamas, alpacas, people, condors, and pumas chasing llamas. Some are a rusty, reddish color. Others are charcoal-gray or white. The paintings are thousands of years old and have been made at different times. They show the hunting and later domestication of llamas—one of the llama paintings has a rope around its neck. The paint colors come from lichens growing on the rock mixed with llama blood or llama bone that was burned and bleached.

These paintings conflict with modern religion. The sites of some rock paintings have names like "devil paintings" and "house of the devil." Missionaries and other zealots have destroyed many of the artifacts by painting or engraving crosses or slogans over them. Although there are over a thousand rock-painting sites, anthropologist Matthias Strecker writes: "The tourist will not be able to see much of the country's many-faceted rock art. Only three sites have so far been declared archaeological parks, protected by fences and controlled by guards. As vandalism has already affected part of the rock art, Bolivian archaeologists are not in favour of tourists visiting other sites." Those three sites are Copacabana, Calacala (near Oruro), and Samaipata (southwest of Santa Cruz). Fortunately, some of the sites are being protected, for example, at Calacala, the German and Dutch governments funded a fence around the site and stairs that prevent visitors from touching the paintings.

Protection of indigenous sites is a challenge to Bolivia. Much of the buildings at Tiwanaku are unexcavated, left underground because the ruins are better protected. The Bolivian government can't afford to protect them with fences and guards if they were unearthed.

There is a story everywhere in Bolivia. One is of the national colors and the national flower, the *kantuta*. As with all Bolivian legends, there are several versions. One tells of an Incan princess

The Bolivian flag. Image © Amihay Shraga

who accompanied her father, the Incan king, to Copacabana near the shores of Lake Titicaca. The princess fell in love with a commoner from a subjugated tribe. Both knew that the pursuit of their love was impossible, since Incan customs would never allow the marriage of a princess with a lowly member of a conquered tribe. The day before the royal entourage departed, the princess slipped away to see the young man, Kento. She slipped down the ravine and left behind her blood on the thorns of a bush. The next morning, the bush flowered with a red blossom. Since it happened near Kento's house, the flower is called *Kantuta*. When mature, the flower points downward from a shrub the size of a small tree. When the flower is not pointing down, it is red at the top, yellow in the middle, and green at the bottom, the colors of the Bolivian flag.

nternational flights arrive in La Paz and Santa Cruz. For either destination, use the web to research the current state of social unrest and road blockades (see news websites on page 115). At worst, roads between the airport and the city will be blockaded. Blockades at La Paz prevent travel on all roads to and from Lake Titicaca, for example.

If you arrive in La Paz, you must plan for high elevation. La Paz lies at 12,000 feet (3,650 m), so visit to your doctor before the trip to get a prescription for high-altitude medication. Coca tea helps a little. Even with the medication, expect to feel sluggish, light-headed, and you may get a mild headache. These symptoms pass within two or three days. One strategy is to immediately head for lower elevation, such as Coroico, over the Road of Death, or to Cochabamba.

The Road of Death

Coroico is a lovely tourist-friendly town at moderate elevation. Small hotels perched on ridges overlook sweeping valleys
filled with lush forest and puffs of clouds. There are many hiking
paths and the town center is a quaint, colonial-style haven. As for
the Road of Death, there is now a new route that forks at Chuspi-
pata, but it's fine to take the original road. Remember that the
many deaths each year occur on overcrowded trucks. A good way
to go is via the minibuses that leave from the Villa Fátima district
in La Paz. You can also bike down the road or arrange a taxi from
La Paz so that you can stop to take pictures.

In La Paz, visit the Coca Museum in the Witchs' Market. The
Coca Museum was started by Dr. Jorge Hurtado, a physician, coca
researcher, and now the head of Bolivia's largest psychiatric hospital.
There, you can buy coca candy to help with *soroche* (altitude sickness) so this is a good place to go right away. The Witchs' Market
sells offerings that the indigenous use at ceremonies: dried llama
fetuses, fake paper money, little vials of liquids that represent health,
good luck in business, or *Pachamama*. You might spot a *yatiri*, an
indigenous priest who diagnoses illnesses and forecasts the future
based on how the coca leaves fall from his hands. Be very careful of
pickpockets on Plaza San Francisco, just below the Witchs' Market.

Other things to see in La Paz include Plaza Murillo. Look for
bullet holes in government buildings that surround the square.
Again, a local guide can explain. For those who love a dramatic
history, read a book on the War of the Pacific (see references) and
then go to the Museo de Litoral. La Paz has other good museums,
including the textile museum, the ethnographic and folklore
museum, and the children's museum. The major cultural event in
La Paz is its carnival, held early in late May or early June.

El Alto, the town above La Paz where the airport is, is the capital of social protest in Bolivia. It is an Aymara city that has seen some
of the world's fastest rates of urban growth. El Alto has huge and
interesting markets, some of which are periodic (Sunday and Thurs-
day), but go with a guide and be careful of pickpockets. You can
arrange a tour of El Alto from any tourist agency in La Paz.

A must-see excursion from La Paz is to Lake Titicaca, accompanied by a boat ride to Isla de la Luna where virgins were raised for sacrifice on neighboring Isla del Sol. Isla del Sol has some comfortable little hotels with spectacular views of Lake Titicaca, and it's a good place to enjoy hiking on trails that include old Incan roads. Take a boat across the lake to Copacabana or Peru. (Do be careful: the tropical sun shining through sparse atmosphere at 12,500 feet [3,800 m], combined with low ozone levels over the lake, readily burns people's retinas, a painful condition prevented by dark glasses and a hat.) In Copacabana, see the Virgin of Copacabana, the most important Bolivian religious symbol, carved by Tito Yupanqui in 1580 and taken as the rallying symbol for indigenous rebellions.

South in the *altiplano* lies Oruro, famous for its annual carnival. Carnival is a deep dip into Bolivian culture—crowds throw water balloons and squirt canned foam at most anyone, especially foreign women. Surrounding Oruro are many interesting mining towns, some just above the city and others southeast at Huanuni, Llallagua, and Uncía. If you want to experience the weft and warp of Bolivia, you must visit mining towns. Read about their difficult histories first and have a guide take you to the sites. It is a powerful experience. Also near Oruro are the rock paintings at Calacala (not to be confused with Cala Cala near Uncía).

Potosí is another must-see in Bolivia. It is reached via Sucre. Take a mine tour in Potosí and visit the royal mint, where the Spanish made the coins that bought them 100 years of empire. Do read about Potosí first too—it will greatly enhance your experience.

Sucre, called The White City, is a beautiful colonial city set on rolling hills, redolent in history. The Casa de la Libertad has a stunning row of portraits of Bolivian presidents, a good way to really experience Bolivian history. The city has many fine Catholic churches, monasteries, and convents.

An unusual excursion is Aerosur's WWII-vintage DC3 flight to Uyuni to stay in the salt hotel. Check for times, as it does not fly all year. Another out-of-the-way trip is to combine southwest

Hotel made of salt found in Salar de Ujuni. Image © Marlyred

Bolivia with the Atacama via a train that runs from Uyuni (or Oruro or Villazón) to Calama in Chile. Again, check for times and availability.

Tarija to the south is a world of its own. With a mild climate, and far removed from the rest of Bolivia, Tarija has wonderful wineries and fossil sites. Above it is the Sama Cordillera Natural Reserve, where you can investigate the ecology of flamingos, see puma tracks, hike Inca roads, and frolic in sand dunes. Historically, Tarija had little mineral wealth, so the Spaniards who came there looked for an agricultural existence. Tarija was not militarized like La Paz and was used to managing their own affairs. A locally famous historical figure, "Moto" (José Eustaquio) Mendez was the hero of a battle against the Spanish royalists, helping to establish the independence of Tarija. At independence, representatives from Tarija were not allowed to vote at the Casa de la Libertad in Sucre, because the rest of Bolivia wasn't sure it was part of the country at all.

Santa Cruz is the capital of the east, a modern city built in rings around an old colonial core. The farther suburban rings look like Southern California, with chic cafés, glassy shops, and Mercedes dealerships. In Santa Cruz, visit CIDAC (the Centro de Investigación, Diseño y Comercialización de la Artesania Cruceño). CIDAC is an example of how artisan communities can become successfully incorporated into economic development projects (see Kevin Healy's book in Further Reading on page 114). The artisan products are fabulous, colorful, and authentic products of several indigenous groups in the department of Santa Cruz, including weaving, pottery, woodcraft, painting, sculpture, and basket weaving.

There is little to see north or east of Santa Cruz except the Jesuit towns. Jesuits were the first Europeans to settle the departments of northern Santa Cruz and Beni, leaving their churches and missions as the sites of today. East of Trinidad at Ibibaté, about 30 miles (50 km), are some of the 60 foot (18 m) high pyramids covered by forest and built largely of broken ceramics.

The department of Pando to the north, like the Beni and northern Santa Cruz, are quite different than the rest of the country, set in the steaming heat of the Amazon jungle. Pando is the site of the rubber and Brazil nut booms. These areas are very remote. Visitors would most likely arrive by air in Riberalta or Guayaramerín and tour the countryside by boat, virtually the only way to travel.

The Chaco to the southwest of Santa Cruz is an enormous, flat, hot combination of near-desert and swamp. The captivating stories there surround Mennonites, the Chaco War (see references), native tribes, and the sometimes extreme evangelization of them. The war sites have mostly disappeared, weathering away under the pressure of agriculture and neglect, but there are a few Chaco War museums in local towns like Villamontes. Few visitors develop the interest to visit such far-flung places, to learn such remote stories. Tarija has an old-folks home for Chaco War veterans, whom you can visit and they will describe their stories.

TIPS FOR TRAVELERS

Climate and Clothing

The basic climatic factor of Bolivia is altitude. All of Bolivia is tropical (a descriptor of latitude), so the sun is always strong, in highlands or lowlands. Use strong sunscreen or you can get severe sunburns, and have dark glasses and a hat always at the ready. Seasonal variation is of rainfall, not temperature. Highlands are always cold at night, and quite dry throughout the year, but are slightly rainier from November to February. It is always rainy in the northeast, and even more so during that same period. The Santa Cruz area is coolest and driest from June to September and quite rainy from November to February. The Chaco is extremely dry except from November to February. It is rather hot throughout the year, but hottest in those same months. The Chaco has the highest recorded temperatures in South America.

Money

Airports have money-changing counters and are quite convenient. The American dollar is the easiest foreign currency to change and is accepted at banks and *casas de cambios*. They will charge a few percent to change traveler's checks. VISA is widely accepted in cities, but don't count on small or rural places taking your credit card, even if the sign on the front door says they will. Hang on to small bills because bigger ones are hard to change. Third-world countries don't print their own money and it costs their federal government a lot of money to have money printed, so they avoid it. Prior to events in Zimbabwe under Robert Mugabe, Bolivia had the world's highest inflation in the 1980s. Bolivia did learn from that, and inflation late in the first decade of the 21st century was only a few percent a year. During the MAS years after 2005, inflation has increased to the high teens.

Safety

Bolivia has the second-lowest crime rate in Latin America, but crime in all Latin American countries is higher than the U.S. Crime in Bolivia is typically petty theft—take precautions in crowded markets, bus stations, and around ATM machines. Violent crime is rare. Avoid all road blockades and street protests. There are tourist police at many bus stations. Inquire locally about safety.

Women Travelers

Bolivia is subject to *machismo*, and women can expect some come-on comments. Modest dress will help to discourage these; follow the style of women you see locally. In the hot lowlands, there are shorts and a more liberal dress code.

Health

Before you leave, get an anti-malarial prescription if you go to the lowlands. You must take it one week prior to arrival. Use the U.S. Center for Disease Control website for other precautions. For *soroche*, get a prescription for high-altitude medication before you arrive. Coca tea will help a little and the symptoms go away in a few days. Expect a slight headache and to become tired quickly.

Souvenirs

What is unique about Bolivia are the crafts and products of indigenous culture. In the highlands these products include textiles, silver jewelry (most of the gold in jewelry is imported), alpaca shawls, and semi-precious stones like serpentine. In the lowlands visit CIDAC, as described in chapter 4. By purchasing indigenous products from local organizations, you send a signal to the market that these things are valued. Seeking out authentic, local artisan products is a good way to support indigenous Bolivians.

Taxis

Taxis are a good way to get around Bolivia. There are, however, different types of taxis. Some are only for your party and will not take on more riders. Such taxis are routinely found at airports and hotels and are usually called radio taxis. Other taxi services may post a destination in the window, will pick up additional riders, and won't give you door-to-door service but drop you near where you want to go instead. Ask at your hotel desk, or a merchant or local, what the fare to your destination should be. Ask the driver first about the fare. If it seems high, it may well be. Bolivian taxis are unionized, so the driver serving the union function may expect you to go in the taxi he points out, but these rules are often ignored.

Local guides

A local guide is an excellent way to get around. Hire them through a local tourist agency and agree on the price beforehand. It is easy to find one who speaks English. If you travel on your own, you must speak some simple, basic Spanish. I highly recommend hiring local guides throughout Bolivia—you learn things you wouldn't otherwise and you get to meet Bolivians.

FURTHER READING
AND BOOKSTORES

De Bonelli, L Hugh. *Travels in Bolivia: with a Tour Across the Pampas to Buenos Ayres &c.* London: Hurst and Blackett, 1854.

Dunkerly, James. *Rebellion in the Veins: Political Struggle in Bolivia, 1952-1982.* London: Thetford Press, 1984.

Estigarriba, José Felix. *The Epic of the Chaco: Marshal Estigarriba's Memoirs of the Chaco War, 1932-1935.* Edited and annotated by Ynsfran, Pablo Max. Austin: University of Texas Press, 1950.

Ferry, Stephen. *I Am Rich Potosí: The Mountain That Eats Men.* New York: The Monacelli Press, 1999.

Fifer, Valerie J. *Bolivia: Land, Location, and Politics Since 1825.* Cambridge: Cambridge University Press, 1972.

Farcau, Bruce W. *The Chaco War: Bolivia and Paraguay, 1932-1925.* Westport, CT: Praeger Publishers, 1996.

———. *The Ten Cents War: Chile, Peru, and Bolivia in the War of the Pacific, 1879-1884.* Westport, CT: Praeger Publishers, 2000.

Healy, Kevin. *Llamas, Weavings, and Organic Chocolate: Multicultural Grassroots Development in the Andes and Amazon of Bolivia.* Indiana: Notre Dame Press, 2001.

Klaiber, Jeffrey. *The Church, Dictatorships, and Democracy in Latin America.* Maryknoll, New York: Orbis Books, 1998.

Levy, Marcela López. *Bolivia.* London: Oxfam, 2001.

Klein, Herbert S. *A Concise History of Bolivia.* Cambridge: Cambridge University Press, 2003.

McFarren, Peter. *Mascaras de los Andes Bolivianos.* La Paz: Editorial Quipus, 1993.

———. *Textiles en los Andes Bolivianos.* La Paz: Fundación Cultural Quipus, 2003.

Mosley, Michael E. *The Incas and Their Ancestors: The Archeology of Peru.* London: Thames and Hudson Ltd., 1992.

Prescott, William Hickling. *History of the Conquest of Peru.* New York : Modern Library, 1998.

Squier, E. George. *Peru: Incidents of Travel and Exploration in the Land of the Incas.* New York: Henry Holt and Company, 1877.

Queiser Morales, Waltraud. *A Brief History of Bolivia*. NY: Facts on File, Inc., 2003.

Quipus Cultural Foundation. *An Insider's Guide to Bolivia*. La Paz, 2003.

Zook, David H., Jr. *The Conduct of the Chaco War*. New Haven, Connecticut: Bookman Associates, 1960.

Local Bookstores

Cochabamba: Los Amigos del Libro, Av. Heroínas 138

La Paz: Los Amigos del Libro, Calle Mercado 1315

Sucre: Lectura, Plaza 25 de Mayo 3

Santa Cruz: Los Amigos del Libro, Calle Ingave 14

Tarija: Cencotar, Av. Domingo Paz O-149

Websites

News:

Note that if you Google these sites, Google will offer to translate them into English.

La Razón (La Paz): **www.la-razon.com**

El Diario (La Paz): **www.eldiario.net**

El Deber (Santa Cruz): www.eldeber.com.bo

Diario Critico de Bolivia (Spain): www.diariocritico.com

Los Tiempos (Cochabamba): www.lostiempos.com

Bolivian Web in English: **www.redbolivia.com/noticias/News** in English

Travel advisories:

U.S. Department of State travel advisories: http://travel.state.gov/travel

U.S. Health travel advisories: wwwn.cdc.gov/travel

General reference:

Organizations, resources, links: **www.lanic.utexas.edu/la/sa/bolivia**

Portal with Bolivian links: www.boliviaweb.com

U.S. CIA World Factbook: www.cia.gov/library/publications/the-world-factbook/geos/bl.html

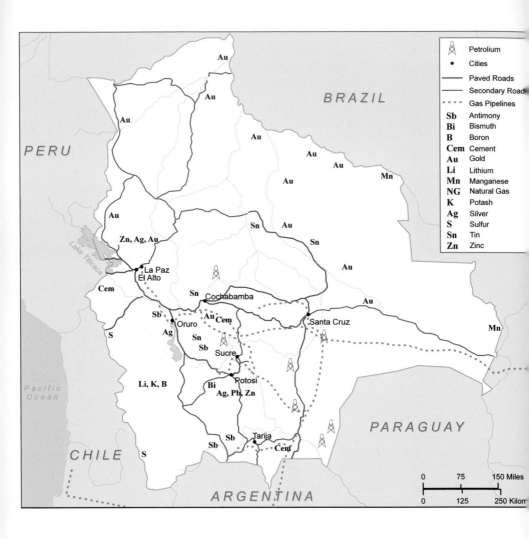

FACTS AND FIGURES

GEOGRAPHY

Official name: República de Bolivia

Situation: lies between latitude 10° S and 23° S and between longitude 58° W and 70° W

Surface area: 424.14 sq mi (1,098.51 sq km) (INE)

Boundaries: total: 4,312 mi (6,940 km) *border countries*: Argentina 832 km, Brazil 3,423 km, Chile 860 km, Paraguay 750 km, Peru 1,075 km (CIA)

Administrative divisions: 9 *departamentos* (by 2001 population size): La Paz (2,350,000), Santa Cruz (2,029,000), Cochabamba (1,456,000), Potosí (709,000), Chuquisaca (531,000), Oruro (392,000), Tarija (391,000), Beni (363,000), Pando (53,000) (INE)

Capital: La Paz is the administrative capital; Sucre is the constitutional capital and has the Supreme Court.

Other large towns: (by population size, 2006 est): **Santa Cruz (1,397,700), La Paz (835,200) El Alto (827,200), Cochabamba (586,800), Sucre (247,300), Oruro (216,600), Tarija (170,900), Potosí (149,200)** (INE)

Infrastructure: paved roads: 3,749 km, unpaved: 58,730 km; railroads: 3,504 km; pipelines: gas 4,860 km, liquid petroleum gas 47 km, oil 2,475 km, refined products 1,589 km, unknown (oil/water) 247 km (2007); airports with paved runways: 16; airports with unpaved runways: 1,045; ports: none (CIA)

Relief and landscape: Western highlands are 35% of land area, at an average elevation of 12,000 ft (3,650 m); Eastern lowlands are 65% of land area, at an average elevation of 1,000 ft (about 300 m).

Climate and vegetation: Highland climates in the *altiplano* are dry and cool; Northern lowland climates are moist and warm; Southern lowland climates in the Chaco are hot and dry. Temperatures vary little across seasons. Rainy season is December to February.

POPULATION

Population: 9.35 million (2008, WHO)

Ethnicity (based on language): 50% indigenous (INE), about 35% mestizo, 15% white

Population growth rate: 1.9% (2008, WB)

Urbanization: 65% (2006, WB)

Fertility: 3.6 (2006, WB)

Age structure: 0-14 years: 33.5%, 15-64 years: 61.8%, 65+ years: 4.7% (CIA)

Birth rate: 22.31 (2008 est., WB)

Mortality rate: 61 (2006, WB)

Infant mortality: 67 (2008, WHO)

Average life expectancy: 65 (2006, WB)

Health care (Public expenditure on health as % of GDP, 2008): 6.9% (WHO)

Literacy rate: 87% (2006, WB)

Education: combined primary, secondary, and tertiary enrollment rate = 86%, or 41st out of 172 countries (UNDP)

Universities: 10 universities. The two oldest, largest, and most well known are the University of San Andrés in La Paz and San Francisco Xavier University in Sucre.

Social development index: UNDP Human Development Index, 2007–2008 = 0.695, or 117th out of 177 countries

Religion: mostly Roman Catholic and syncretic mix with indigenous religions, but with growth of evangelical churches

Languages: Spanish, Quechua, Aymara

Notes:

    INE = Instituto Nacional Estadística de Bolivia

    WB = World Bank

    CIA = Central Intelligence Agency

    UNDP = United Nations Development Program

    WHO = World Health Organization

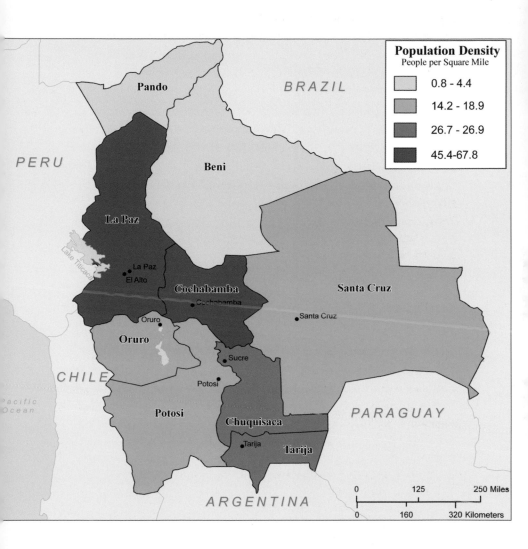

Population Density
People per Square Mile

- 0.8 - 4.4
- 14.2 - 18.9
- 26.7 - 26.9
- 45.4-67.8

BRAZIL

PERU

Pando

Beni

La Paz

La Paz
El Alto

Lake Titicaca

Cochabamba
Cochabamba

Oruro

Oruro

Santa Cruz

Santa Cruz

CHILE

Pacific
Ocean

Sucre

Potosi

Potosi

Chuquisaca

PARAGUAY

Tarija
Tarija

ARGENTINA

| 0 | 125 | 250 Miles |
| 0 | 160 | 320 Kilometers |

HISTORY AND POLITICS

Key historical dates: * 10,000 BCE: arrival of man in the Andes * 2500 BCE: settled agriculture with increasing population, societal organization, and labor specialization * 1000 BCE: Wankarani * 800–100 BCE: Chavín * 700 BCE–50 CE: Chiripa * 500 BCE–200 CE: Pukara * 100 BCE–1200 CE: Tiwanaku civilization dominates the *altiplano*, known for terraced farming, temple building, irrigation, roads, pottery, and development of bronze * 1200–1460: Aymara Kingdoms * 1400s–1532: Inca civilization absorbs other *altiplano* groups * 1532: arrival of Spaniards * 1533: death of Atahualpa * 1533–1825: Spanish colonial period * 1570–1650: silver boom in Potosí * 1780–1782: rebellion of Túpac Amaru * 1809: death of Pedro Domingo Murillo * 1810–1825: the Fifteen Years War of independence against Spain *1825: Bolivian independence * 1825–1828: presidency of José Antonio de Sucre * 1929–1839: presidency of Andrés Santa Cruz * 1841–1880: the *caudillos* * 1864–1870: dictatorship of Mariano Melgarejo * 1876–1880: dictatorship of Hilarión Daza * 1879–1884: the War of the Pacific * 1880–1899: Bolivia's biggest silver boom * 1900: transition from silver to tin * 1920s: decline of tin * 1932–1935: the Chaco War * 1936–1946: formation of political parties and growth of national socialism * 1946–1952: return of the *rosca* * 1952–1964: Victor Paz Estenssoro's national revolution * 1964–1982: military governments, including 1964–1969: René Barrientos, 1971–1978: Hugo Banzer, and 1980–1981: Garcia Meza * 1967: Ché Guevara killed in Bolivia * 1951–1983: Klaus Barbie in Bolivia * 1982–present: democracy * 1985–1989: Paz Estenssoro's third term * 1993–1997: Gonzalo Sánchez de Lozada's first term * 1994: Popular Participation Laws *1997–2001: Hugo Banzer's second term * 2001–2003: Sánchez de Lozada's second term * 2003–2005: Carlos Mesa and later, Chief Justice as temporary presidents * 2005–present: Evo Morales and his socialist MAS party

ECONOMY

Gross Domestic Product: $39.44 billion (2007 est., CIA)
GDP/capita (PPP): $4,000 (2007 est., CIA), $4,013 (2007 est., IMF), $4,208 (2007 est., WB)
Unit of currency: Boliviano (8 Bolivianos = $1 U.S., August, 2008)
Inflation: 8.7% (2007 est., CIA). Forecasts are for higher inflation.
GDP growth: 2.9% 1996–2006; 4.0% forecast growth 2006–2010
GDP by sector: agriculture 14%, industry 34%, services 52%
Debt: $4.492 billion (31 December 2007 est., CIA)
Debt as percent of GDP: 46.6% (2007 est., CIA)
Economic aid: $582.9 million (2005 est., CIA)
Income distribution (Gini coefficient): 59.2 (the poorest 10% of Bolivians earn 0.3% of GDP; the richest 10% earn 47%) (2002, CIA)
Unemployment: 7.5% in urban areas; widespread underemployment (2007 est., CIA)
Exports: natural gas, soybeans and soy products, crude petroleum, zinc ore, tin (2006, CIA)
Imports: petroleum products, plastics, paper, aircraft and aircraft parts, prepared foods, automobiles, insecticides, soybeans (2006, CIA)
Principal export partners: Brazil 45.5%, Argentina 9.2%, US 8.7%, Colombia 6.8%, Japan 6.7%, South Korea 4.3% (2006, CIA)
Principal import partners: Brazil 29.5%, Argentina 16.2%, Chile 10.3%, U.S. 9.5%, Peru 8% (2006, CIA)

BOLIVIA AND THE UNITED STATES

U.S. aid to Bolivia, not counting coca interdiction, is about $85 million. It is channeled through USAID and implemented by NGOs, the private sector, and the Bolivian government. Targets of USAID are food aid ($32 million), child health ($18 million), development assistance ($12 million), economic support ($12 million), Peace Corps ($3 million), and military financing ($3 million). (2003, U.S. Department of State)

.S. supports with $91 million coca eradication and interdic-
..., the interception of smuggled coca leaf and the chemicals used
to make cocaine. That aid is channeled to an arm of the Bolivian
military (2003, U.S. Department of State).

The U.S. is not one of Bolivia's main trading partners, compared
to Brazil and Argentina, nor is it one of the top aid donors if
money directed to coca eradication is taken out. The E.U. (lumped
together), Japan, and China all give Bolivia large amounts of
foreign aid. Yet the political influence of the U.S. is quite strong,
in part because of U.S. support in the contentious areas of coca,
financing and training for the military, and vocal weighing-in for
or against what Bolivians see as their own internal politics.

Ponchos in Tarabuco Market. Image © Morton Elm

GLOSSARY

Cambas	The Bolivian word for highlanders. See *Kollas*.
Caudillo	A strongman, a dictator, especially applied to the period 1841–1880.
Cholita	An adult indigenous female.
Creole	In most Latin American history, a Creole is a person of Spanish parents born in the New World.
Campesino	A name created in 1952, under Paz's socialism, to give dignity to natives, from the *campo* (countryside).
Cholo	An adult indigenous male, more often called a *campesino*.
Departamento	Administrative units that are called states or provinces in North America.
Kollas	The Bolivian word for lowlanders. See *Cambas*.
Leija	Usually made from burnt vegetables such as grain or banana, *lejia* releases the trace amounts of cocaine alkaloid in coca leaf.
Mestizo	Typically in Latin America, *Mestizo* refers to the mixed blood of natives and Europeans. In Bolivia, *Mestizo* is less a reference to race or ethnicity and more an amalgam of dress, urban residence, speaking of Spanish, and having a job in the western-style economy.

A tax paid in labor, begun by native peoples and continued by Spain. Abolished by law by Bolivar, indigenous labor obligation was again officially revoked in 1943 and functionally ended only in 1952.

Soroche   High-altitude sickness. Symptoms are light-headedness, tiring easily, and maybe some nausea. The best remedy is a prescription prior to arrival. Coca tea helps a little; coca candy a bit more.

Yungas   The eastern slope of the Andes, east of La Paz. The traditional home of most of Bolivia's coca, often called "the cloud forest."